HIKING MID-MISSOURI
Scenic Trails of the Heartland

Other Books from Willow Press:

Hiking Ohio, Scenic Trails of the Buckeye State
Hiking Kentucky, Scenic Trails of the Bluegrass State
Walking the Denver-Boulder Region
A Birder's Guide to the Cincinnati Tristate
Birding the Front Range
Colorado's Year
A Guide to American Zoos & Aquariums

About the Authors:

Darcy & Robert Folzenlogen are physicians and naturalists. They have written a number of outdoor guides, including those listed above. All of their books are dedicated to the themes of open space protection, historic preservation and wildlife conservation.

Cover Photos (clockwise from top):

Graham Cave
Autumn at Little Dixie Lake
Rocky Fork Lakes Conservation Area
Grindstone Creek

HIKING MID-MISSOURI
Scenic Trails of the Heartland

by Darcy & Robert Folzenlogen

WILLOW PRESS
Columbia, Missouri
Littleton, Colorado

ISBN: 1-893111-01-6
Library of Congress Card Number: 00-108099

Publisher: **Willow Press**
                Columbia, Missouri
                Littleton, Colorado
                email: willowpress@eudoramail.com

Printed by: John S. Swift Co., Inc.
                Cincinnati, Ohio
                U.S.A.

Photos by Darcy & Robert Folzenlogen
Maps by Robert Folzenlogen, adapted from those provided
        by Missouri Department of Conservation, Missouri
        State Parks, Mark Twain National Forest and the
        National Wildlife Refuge System.

For Sarah, Zach & Ally

ACKNOWLEDGEMENTS

Our sincere thanks to the many park rangers, conservation managers, naturalists and secretaries who took the time to provide us with background information for this guide. Special thanks to the Missouri Department of Conservation, Missouri State Parks, Mark Twain National Forest and Swan Lake National Wildlife Refuge for their research materials and maps.

Our thanks to Jan Jolley and her associates at John S. Swift Co., Inc., for their creative advice and technical assistance.

A special and heartfelt thanks to the many Conservation Organizations and individuals who, over the years, have worked to protect Missouri' s natural heritage. Without their devotion, we hikers and naturalists would not be able to enjoy the many open space preserves that fill this guide. We encourage all of our readers to advance the cause of Missouri's conservation community by donating time and/or money to the organizations listed in Appendix II of this book.

Finally, our love and thanks to Sarah, Zach and Ally for their support and understanding.

- Darcy & Robert Folzenlogen

CONTENTS

(CONTINUED)

INTRODUCTION

Blending the Glaciated Plains with the Ozark Highlands and bisected by the broad valley of the Missouri River, Mid Missouri offers a scenic wonderland for hikers, naturalists and weekend explorers. This guide describes 122 dayhikes at 40 areas throughout central Missouri, chosen to depict the topographic, geologic, floral and faunal diversity of the region.

Each hiking area is illustrated with maps and photos and a narrative describes the natural and historic features that characterize the preserve. Trail mileage, terrain, difficulty and walking time are provided for each hike.

Section I provides an overview of Missouri's landscape while Appendix I offers a synopsis of the State's geologic and natural history. Appendix II lists regional conservation organizations that are working to protect Missouri's natural heritage; their work is vital to the health of the State's open spaces and your support for their efforts is strongly encouraged.

HIKING SEASON

To fully appreciate the beauty and diversity of our natural areas, one should visit during each season of the year. Indeed, all seasons yield special rewards for those who explore the State's wild lands. Autumn colors paint the landscape and migrant waterfowl fill the wetlands in October and November. Winter brings the peaceful, snow-laden forest and is perhaps the best season for observing Missouri's raptors and carnivores. March brings another tide of migrants to the State's lakes and reservoirs while April wildflowers carpet the forest floor. Warblers entice the birdwatchers in early May and, by mid spring, the woods and meadows are alive with the sights and sounds of a new generation. Summer heat dries and dims the landscape but grassland wildflowers provide a spectacular backdrop as the season wanes.

Novice hikers often confine their adventures to the warm months of spring and summer. In doing so, they experience the crowds and insects while missing some of nature's more rewarding displays.

Those hoping to observe resident wildlife should plan their excursion for the early morning or late daylight hours; birds and mammals tend to be most active, and thus most visible, during those times of day.

WHAT TO BRING

The most important requirement for any outdoor adventure is a companion who can go for help should an accident occur. While many of us enjoy the solitude that nature affords, an unexpected injury can prove to be fatal, especially during the winter months.

Layered clothing will permit adjustment to changing weather conditions and sturdy, waterproof boots are a must for the serious hiker. Be sure to bring plenty of water and high-energy snacks for the longer trips and a waterproof parka will combat hypothermia when rain or snow develop. Insect repellant is highly recommended from April through October; be sure to check yourself for ticks at the end of the day.

Binoculars will add to your enjoyment of wildlife and vistas. Naturalists will also want to bring along field guides which depict the flora and fauna native to Missouri; some of these are listed in the Bibliography of this book.

STATE CONSERVATION AREAS

Many of the hiking locations included in this guide are State Conservation Areas. While these preserves are excellent destinations for day hikes and nature study, they do not offer the "comfort facilities" and manicured trails of State and County Parks. Furthermore, seasonal hunting is permitted on these lands and many of the wetland areas are closed in winter to provide refuge for waterfowl.

For your safety, we advise that you avoid these areas during the deer and turkey hunting seasons. If you are unsure regarding the hunting dates, contact the Missouri Department of Conservation (Appendix II).

LOW IMPACT HIKING

When visiting the nature preserves of Missouri, *take only pictures and leave only footprints*. Be sure to pack out any trash that you may produce on your hike and pick up any that you might encounter along the trail.

By staying on designated trails, your impact on the local ecology will be minimized. Native flora should be left undisturbed and resident wildlife should be viewed from a safe and non-threatening distance. Plan to leave your dog at home; dogs often harass wildlife and disturb other hikers.

Finally, help to protect what remains of the State's natural heritage by donating time and/or money to the conservation organizations listed in Appendix II of this guide; their work is vital to the future welfare of our many preserves and parklands.

- Darcy & Robert Folzenlogen

KEY TO THE MAPS

Roads:

Parking Areas:

Trails:

Bridges/Boardwalks:

Stairs:

Powerlines:

Lakes/Streams:

Marsh:

Forest/Woodlands:

Rock Outcrop/Cliff:

Viewpoint/Overlook:

I. THE LANDSCAPE OF MID-MISSOURI

In Central Missouri, the relatively flat Glaciated Plain of the Upper Midwest blends with the rugged hills of the Ozark Uplift. This varied topography is further sculpted by the Missouri River and its many tributaries, creating a superb diversity of natural habitat.

THE GLACIATED PLAIN

Continental ice sheets pushed southward across Canada and the northern United States at least four times during the last two million years; commonly known as the "Ice Age," this was the Pleistocene Epoch of geologic time. The last ice advance, the Wisconsin Glaciation, expanded from eastern Canada some 70,000 years ago, scouring the landscape and enriching the soil with glacial till. As it retreated northward, 10-15,000 years ago, it left behind moraines of gravel, erratic boulders, a myriad of glacial lakes (including the Great Lakes) and a rich bed of loam.

Prior to the arrival of white explorers and settlers, the Glaciated Plain was covered by a vast tallgrass prairie. High winds, periods of drought, prairie wildfires and huge herds of bison kept the forest at bay and trees were confined primarily to the stream beds and river valleys. Converted to the "Corn Belt" by modern Americans, the Glaciated Plain is now a mosaic of croplands, ranches and cities.

Most of Northern Missouri lies within this geophysical region. Rock outcrops, found primarily along streams, are of Pennsylvanian age in northwest and north-central Missouri while Mississippian rocks are exposed across the Salt River valley of northeast Missouri. The land is flat to gently rolling, with only modest relief along the major streams.

Resident mammals include white-tailed deer, red fox, coyotes, badgers, cottontail rabbits, skunk, prairie voles, deer mice, Franklin's and thirteen-lined ground squirrels, southern bog lemmings and meadow jumping mice. Preying on many of the smaller mammals are northern harriers, red-tailed hawks, American kestrels, barn owls and great-horned owls. The songbird population is characterized by eastern meadowlarks, dickcissels, eastern bluebirds, barn swallows, American crows, mourning doves, northern bobwhites and a variety of sparrows. Massasauga rattlesnakes are among the prairie reptiles.

Of course, man has altered the landscape with dams, lakes and reservoirs, producing new habitats for wildlife. These man-made wetlands attract migrant waterfowl, bald eagles, ospreys, white pelicans, gulls, terns, herons, egrets and Mississippi kites. Migrant shorebirds can be abundant on the lakeshore mudflats. Red-headed woodpeckers and belted kingfishers are common in the drowned woodlands and both beaver and muskrat utilize the ponds and lakes.

4

THE OZARK UPLIFT

The highlands of northern Arkansas and southern Missouri are composed of an uplifted plateau that has been carved into a maze of hills and valleys by the tributaries of the Arkansas and Missouri Rivers. The rock layers of this plateau, deposited in shallow Paleozoic seas, have remained horizontal, forming outcrops along creeks, rivers and roadways. Mississippian limestone of the Burlington Formation is exposed throughout much of Boone County while Ordovician rocks predominate south of the Missouri River. A dome of Precambrian granite in southeast Missouri has been sculpted into the Francois Mountains, the highest summits in our State.

In areas where relatively insoluble rock overlies thick beds of limestone or dolomite, cave formations and springs are numerous. Surface water leaks through fissures in the caprock and, over thousands of years, dissolves channels in the underlying limestone/dolomite. Such caverns are abundant throughout central and southern Missouri, making our State second only to Tennessee in its number of caves.

In other regions, where flat beds of limestone lie just below the surface, a karst landscape develops with numerous sinkholes and few streams. Where streams do occur, natural bridges are often found. Spectacular examples of karst topography can be found at Rock Bridge State Park (Hiking Area #21) and at Ha Ha Tonka State Park (Hiking Area #38).

The natural bridge at Ha Ha Tonka State Park

5

The dry, rocky soil of the Ozark Plateau is cloaked by a vast forest of oak, hickory and pine. Water-loving trees, such as American sycamore, river birch, maples and poplars cluster along the stream beds. Resident mammals include white-tailed deer, gray fox, bobcats, opossums, raccoons, eastern woodrats, white-footed mice, gray and fox squirrels and eastern chipmunks. Black bear are found in some areas and a small number of mountain lions may still inhabit the plateau. Wild turkey, pileated woodpeckers, broad-winged hawks, turkey vultures, thrushes, nuthatches, titmice and warblers characterize the bird population. Timber rattlesnakes, Osage copperheads and western pygmy rattlesnakes all haunt the woodlands.

THE MISSOURI RIVER VALLEY

The course of the Missouri River was established by the Illinoian Glacier which spread across the northern Plains 400,000 years ago. The River's broad floodplain attests to its tremendous flow during the Pleistocene Epoch and to the force of periodic floods since that time. Young deposits of sand, silt and gravel are spread across the floodplain while older bluffs of Paleozoic rock rise above its sinuous course. The latter are topped by deep coat of glacial loess in western and central Missouri.

The map on page 7 depicts the major streams of central Missouri. With the exception of the Salt River watershed in the northeast, all streams drain toward the Missouri River.

The River and its floodplain wetlands attract huge flocks of waterfowl, American white pelicans, white-faced ibis, gulls, terns and shorebirds during migrations. Egrets, herons, rails and bitterns haunt its marshy shallows during much of the year. Beaver, muskrat and river otters ply the Missouri's tributaries while belted kingfishers, bald eagles and migrant ospreys hunt along its shores. Floodplain woodlands attract raccoons, eastern kingbirds, barred owls, red-headed woodpeckers, cuckoos and flycatchers. Soft-shelled turtles bask on the riverbanks and snapping turtles patrol the shallows.

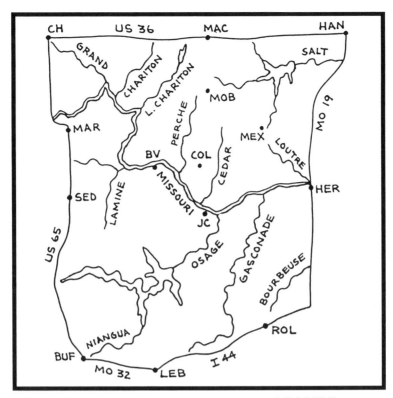

THE STREAMS OF MID MISSOURI

The Missouri River at Eagle Bluffs

7

II. HIKING AREAS OF MID MISSOURI

There are numerous hiking opportunities in Central Missouri. We chose the areas listed below with the goal of covering a wide variety of natural landscape, thereby demonstrating the biologic diversity of our region. The total area covered by this guide is bounded by U.S. 36 on the north, U.S. 65 on the west, MO 32 and I-44 on the south and State Route 19 on the east. The overview map on page 9 notes the general location of these areas; more specific directions are provided in each chapter.

1. Fountain Grove C.A.
2. Pershing S.P.
3. Swan Lake N.W. R.
4. Grand Pass C.A.
5. Van Meter S. P.
6. Arrow Rock S.H.S.
7. Thomas Hill Reservoir C.A.
8. Rudolf Bennitt C.A.
9. Mark Twain Lake & Vicinity
10. Robert White II C.A.
11. Franklin Island C. A.
12. Davisdale C.A.
13. Rocky Fork Lakes C.A.
14. Whetstone Creek C.A.
15. Graham Cave. S.P.
16. Danville C.A.
17. Little Dixie Lake C.A.
18. Bear Creek Trail
19. Grindstone Nature Area
20. MKT Trail

21. Eagle Bluffs C.A.
22. Rock Bridge Memorial S.P.
23. Gans Creek Wild Area
24. Three Creeks C.A.
25. Cedar Creek District, MTNF
26. Katy Trail
27. Bothwell Lodge S.H.S.
28. Prairie Home C.A.
29. Scrivner Road C.A.
30. Runge Conservation N.C.
31. Painted Rock C.A.
32. Ben Branch Lake C.A.
33. Big Buffalo Creek C.A.
34. Saline Valley C.A.
35. Spring Creek Gap C.A.
36. Canaan C.A.
37. Lake of the Ozarks S.P.
38. Ha Ha Tonka S.P.
39. Lead Mine C.A.
40. Bennett Spring S.P.

C.A. -Conservation Area
S.P. - State Park
N.W.R. - National Wildlife Refuge

S.H.S. - State Historic Site
MTNF - Mark Twain Nat. Forest

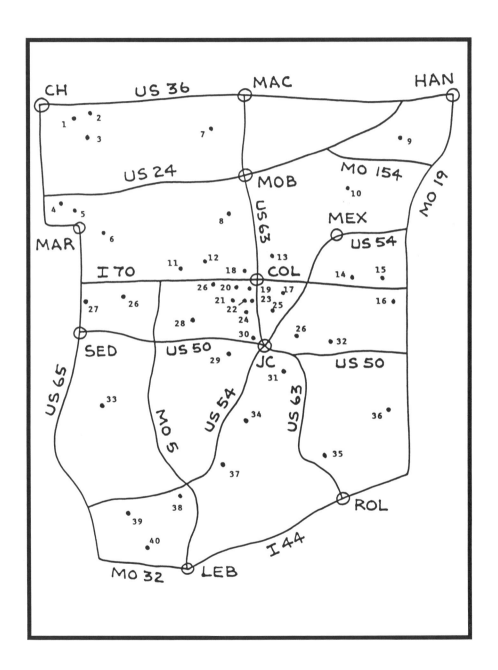

1 FOUNTAIN GROVE CONSERVATION AREA

DISTANCE: DAYHIKES OF 2-8 MILES
TERRAIN: FLAT
DIFFICULTY: EASY
WALKING TIME: 1.5 TO 5 HRS.

Laced with ponds, sloughs, lakes and marshlands, **Fountain Grove Conservation Area** is located at the confluence of Locust Creek and the Grand River. This 7154 acre preserve was developed in the 1940s, the first wetland area of the Missouri Conservation Commission.

The refuge attracts large flocks of wintering and migrant waterfowl and is an excellent place to observe bald eagles during the colder months. Beaver and river otter can also be found here. Great blue herons inhabit the area throughout the year and are joined by a variety of egrets, herons and rails during the summer. Huge flocks of snow geese pass through the area during migrations and are best observed in late February or early March.

Trails run atop levees which divide the numerous lakes, ponds and marshlands; these elevated walkways are relatively dry and provide excellent viewpoints for birdwatching.

Directions: From U.S. 36, just south of Meadville, turn south on Route W and drive 3 miles to Belt Road. Turn left (east) and proceed 1 mile to Crown Rd. Turn right (south) on Crown and proceed to parking areas illutrated on the map. The best hiking opportunities are east of Crown Road and can be accessed from lots P1 and P2.

Routes: One can use the numerous levees and graveled roadways to complete a variety of dayhikes.

We suggest a **2-mile loop** which begins at P2. A levee trail leads northeast along the course of Locust Creek, crossing floodplain woodlands and wet meadows. Approximately 1 mile from the lot, a bridge will be noted on your right; the trail which crosses Hickory Branch via this bridge is the western end of the **Riparian Trail**, a path that originates in Pershing State Park (see next chapter). Bypass this junction and proceed to the next intersection where a levee angles back to the southwest and takes you across open wetlands to the P2 lot (see arrows on map).

A **3-mile hike** begins at lot P1. Hike southward along the east shore of Che-Ru Lake and then follow the arrows on the map. The levees in this area lead past a variety of wetland habitats, from open lake waters to bottomland timber. This insures a diversity of scenery and wildlife.

Gravel roads and levees cross the wetlands

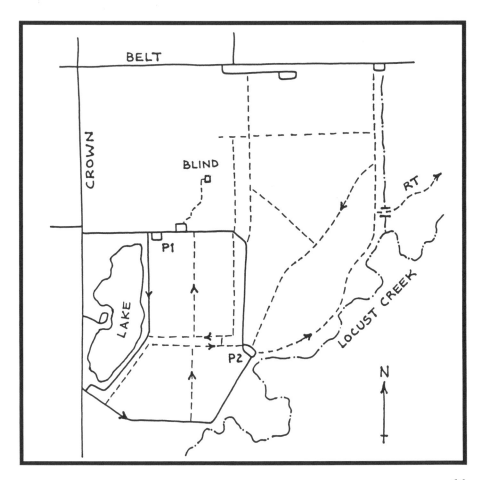

2 PERSHING STATE PARK

BOARDWALK TRAIL
  DISTANCE: 1.5 MILE
  TERRAIN: FLAT
  DIFFICULTY: EASY
  WALKING TIME: 1 HR.

RIPARIAN TRAIL
  DISTANCE: 6 MILES RT
  TERRAIN: FLAT
  DIFFICULTY: EASY
  WALKING TIME: 4 HRS.

Named for General John J. Pershing, a WWI hero who grew up in the area, **Pershing State Park** now encompasses 2335 acres along the course of Locust Creek. The Woodland Grist Mill operated here from 1878 into the early 1900s and Locust Creek is one of only a few large streams in northern Missouri that have not been channelized.

Annual flooding along the stream has created a magnificent bottom-land forest of cottonwood, river birch, pin oak, silver maple and swamp white oak; this woodland has been designated a State Natural Area and is home to barred owls, red-headed woodpeckers and belted kingfishers. River otters inhabit the creek and the rare ostrich fern thrives in this shaded wetland.

Pershing State Park also boasts a 1040 acre wet prairie characterized by cordgrass, big bluestem, smartweed, compass plant and prairie blazing star. Protected from cultivation by frequent floods along Locust Creek, the prairie is now maintained by controlled burns which keep the forest and non-native plants at bay.

Directions: From U.S. 36, 10 miles west of Brookfield, turn south on Missouri 130 which enters the State Park. Hikers should proceed to the drive which angles to the southwest from the campground area; this road is across Route 130 from the Park Office and leads down to a parking area on the east bank of Locust Creek.

Routes: From the parking lot, cross Locust Creek via a bridge and turn left to access the Park's fine **Boardwalk**. This elevated, 1.5 mile route winds through the floodplain woodland and loops out to an **observation tower (T)** on the wet prairie. Turkey vultures and red-tailed hawks often soar above the grassland while great blue herons and American bitterns stalk the marshy shallows.

The **Riparian Trail (RT)**, dedicated in the spring of 2000, begins at the south end of the boardwalk loop. This earthen path is blazed with yellow markers and follows the course of Locust Creek, eventually ending in Fountain Grove Conservation Area (see previous chapter). The round-trip distance to the State Park boundary is 6 miles.

12

The Park's boardwalk snakes across the floodplain

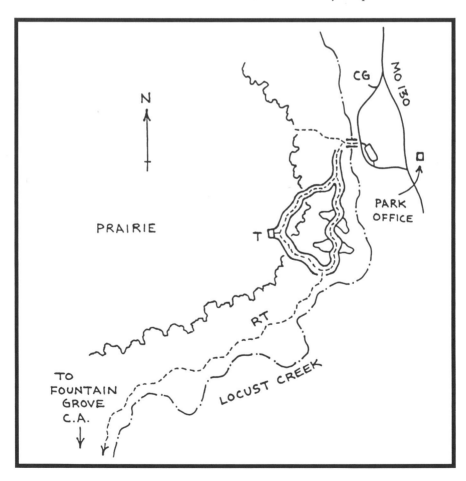

3 SWAN LAKE NATIONAL WILDLIFE REFUGE

DISTANCE: VARIABLE
TERRAIN: FLAT
DIFFICULTY: EASY
WALKING TIME: VARIABLE

Conceived by the Administration of President Theodore Roosevelt, the National Wildlife Refuge System now boasts over 500 nature preserves throughout the United States. Most of these are aligned along the four primary "flyways" of North America, ensuring vital wetlands for migratory waterfowl, while others were established to protect habitat for threatened wildlife species. One of these preserves, **Swan Lake National Wildlife Refuge**, lies within central Missouri.

Established in 1937 to provide migratory and wintering habitat for waterfowl, the Swan Lake Refuge is characterized by two large lakes (Swan Lake and Silver Lake) which are surrounded by wet prairie and seasonal marshlands. Bottomland forest along Yellow Creek adds to the region's diversity; this timbered area is accessed via the Yellow Creek Conservation Area, southwest of Swan Lake.

The refuge is renowned for its large winter population of Canada geese which now number over 200,000. Snow geese are also common during migrations and bald eagles are frequent visitors, especially from November through March. Other resident wildlife include beaver, muskrat and ring-necked pheasant; herons, egrets, rails, American white pelicans and Mississippi kites are among the summer visitors.

Directions: Swan Lake National Wildlife Refuge is best accessed from Route CC, 1.8 miles north of Mendon, or from Route RA, at its junction with County Road 114, south of Sumner.

Routes: By using the graveled roadways and levees of Swan Lake National Wildlife Refuge, dayhikers can cover a variety of distances; sectional mileages are noted on the map.

We suggest a **7 mile loop hike**, south of the Refuge Headquarters. Park near the Headquarters building (HQ) and hike southeastward along the roadway. Turn left at the road junction, eventually crossing a southern arm of **Swan Lake**. Once past the Lake, continue eastward atop a levee (see arrows).

Turn southward above the west shore of **Silver Lake**. Another mile brings you to another levee which angles southwestward toward Yellow Creek; this path intersects a graveled road (see map). Turn right along this road and pick up another levee which skirts the **South Lake Marsh** and eventually merges with a roadway. Continue northward on this road to the Refuge Headquarters.

Refuge lakes attract huge flocks of waterfowl

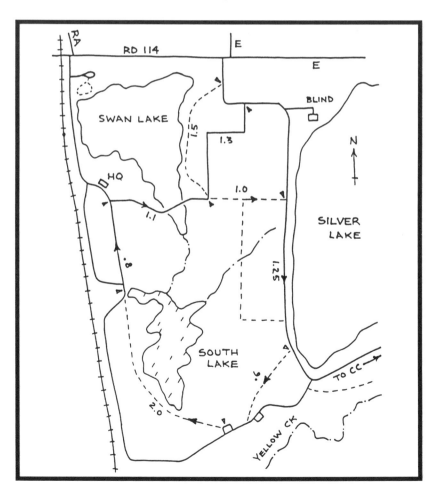

4 GRAND PASS CONSERVATION AREA

DISTANCE: VARIABLE
TERRAIN: FLAT
DIFFICULTY: EASY
WALKING TIME: VARIABLE

Tucked into a bend of the Missouri River, **Grand Pass Conservation Area** is an excellent destination for hikers and naturalists alike. Its 5296 acres stretch across the River's floodplain, creating and protecting a rich mosaic of seasonal wetlands, wet prairies and shallow pools. Earthen and graveled levees criss-cross the preserve, offering access to hunters, hikers and birdwatchers. Western and eastern sections of the area are closed from October 15 to January 15, providing refuge for wintering waterfowl.

March and November bring large flocks of geese and ducks to the area while shorebirds peak in late April and early September. American white pelicans, white-faced ibis, terns and American coot are among the other migrants. Great blue herons are common here throughout the year while summer visitors include great and cattle egrets, green-backed herons, black-crowned night herons, American bitterns and Mississippi kites. Northern harriers and red-tailed hawks patrol the refuge throughout the year, joined by bald eagles during the colder months.

Directions: From Marshall, drive northwest on U.S. 65 for approximately 9 miles. Turn north on Route N and proceed another 6 miles to the Conservation Area. Parking areas are shown on the map.

Routes: A wide variety of dayhikes can be planned using the roadways and levees of Grand Pass Conservation Area; sectional mileages are shown on the map.

Most of the routes cross open country and yield broad views of the wetlands and grasslands that characterize the preserve. Of note is a 1.2 mile trail that leads through bottomland forest at the western edge of the refuge (see map).

16

Shallow pools and wetlands line the roadways

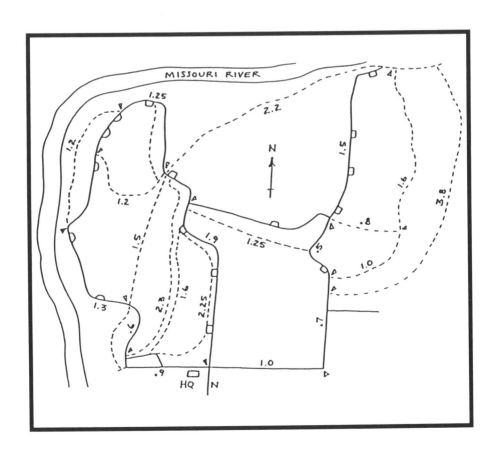

5 VAN METER STATE PARK

RIDGE LOOP
  DISTANCE: 1.7 MILES
  TERRAIN: STEEP HILLS
  DIFFICULTY: MODERATE
  WALKING TIME: 1.5 HRS

LAKE LOOP
  DISTANCE: 1.5 MILES
  TERRAIN: ROLLING, HILLS
  DIFFICULTY: MODERATE
  WALKING TIME: 1 HR.

Draped across a wooded ridge known as "The Pinnacles," **Van Meter State Park** is rich in both scenic beauty and human history. Rising above the Missouri River valley, the ridge is the former home of the Missouri Indians, an agricultural tribe that also hunted bison and conducted trade along the River and its tributaries. Contacted by French explorers in the 1670s, the Missouri Indians were decimated by smallpox within a century.

The Van Meter family settled on the Pinnacles in 1834 and the land was deeded to the State of Missouri by Annie Van Meter in 1932; the family cemetery (C) remains on Park property. Plan to visit the Nature Center before your hike; the building houses displays which depict both the natural and the human history of this area.

Directions: From Marshall, drive north on Missouri Route 41. Proceed approximately 7 miles and turn left (west) on Missouri Route 122. Follow this road for 5 miles to Van Meter State Park.

Routes: The **Ridge Loop (RL)** begins at the Park's picnic area. Cross the creek via a footbridge and turn left. The trail soon curves eastward to cross a stream and then begins a steady climb onto the ridge; watch for wild turkeys that often feed along the path. Exiting the forest, you are at the south end of the **Old Fort**, thought to be an Indian ceremonial site. Hike through the Old Fort and continue down to the **Mounds** area; the burial mounds found here likely predate the modern Missouri Indians and may have been constructed by the Hopewell culture some 800 years ago.

Backtrack through the Old Fort and pick up the east arm of the Ridge Loop (RL), winding through the forest and paralleling the Park road. Bypass a cutoff on your right and continue a gradual descent to the picnic area. Your loop hike has covered 1.7 miles.

The **Lake Loop (1.5 miles)** circles Lake Wooldridge at the north end of the Park road. The route alternately runs along the shoreline and cuts away to cross the feeder streams.

Energetic hikers may want to **combine the above hikes**, using the Park road as a connector. This will yield a total hike of 4.5 miles.

Lake Wooldridge

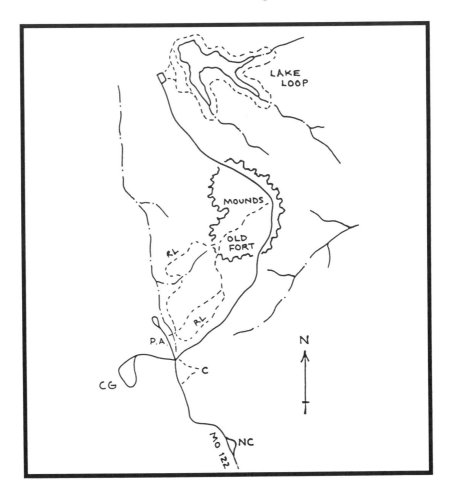

6 ARROW ROCK STATE HISTORIC SITE

DISTANCE: 1.5 MILES
TERRAIN: ROLLING; SOME HILLS
DIFFICULTY: EASY
WALKING TIME: 1 HR.

Commanding a broad view of the Missouri River and its valley, the **Arrow Rock State Historic Site** commemorates a reststop of the Lewis & Clark Expedition on their journey to the West. The Site is also the home of a Boy Scout Camp and harbors a small fishing lake.

A 1.5 mile trail loops through the area and is best accessed at the overlook (V).

Directions: From I-70, take Exit 98 and head north on Missouri 41. Drive 12.3 miles across rolling farmlands to the Historic Site, on your right. Enter the Park, pass the lake and bear left at the intersection; proceed to the overlook area as illustrated on the map.

Route: Arrow Rock's **overlook (V)** yields a magnificent view of the Missouri River valley to the northeast. After enjoying this vista, pick up the trail to your right, entering the forest and undulating to the south, crossing several drainages. The trail soon passes through the east end of a park road and then re-enters the forest.

Curving westward, the path negotiates two more sidestreams and then circles behind the **Boy Scout Campground (CG)**. Bypass connector paths which lead into the campground and continue on the main trail which turns northward and leads above the east shore of the Park's lake. The route soon crosses the entry road and descends along a creek (see map).

Angling to the east, the trail makes two road crossings and then begins a short but steep climb back to the overlook (V).

20

The Missouri River Valley from Arrow Rock

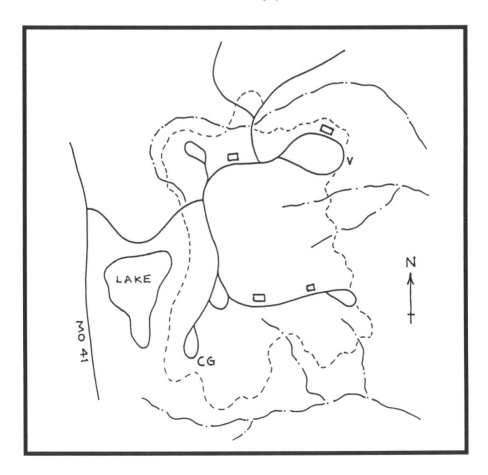

7 THOMAS HILL CONSERVATION AREA

DISTANCE: ALL LESS THAN 2 MILES
DIFFICULTY: EASY TO MODERATE
TERRAIN: ROLLING TO HILLY
WALKING TIME: ALL LESS THAN 1.5 HRS.

Thomas Hill Reservoir is a 4950 acre lake on the Little Chariton River in north-central Missouri. The southern end of the reservoir is bordered by a large mining operation and a power plant. The rest of the lake is rimmed by the **Thomas Hill Conservation Area**, a narrow band of meadows, marshlands, riparian woodlands and upland forest.

Hiking opportunities are rather limited here but the varied habitats make the area an interesting destination for naturalists. Of special interest is the backwater (northern) zone where beaver activity is evident and where seasonal mudflats and shallows attract a variety of migrant shorebirds, pelicans and waders. Bald eagles and ospreys often visit the reservoir and the backwater wetlands host an assortment of wildlife. Drowned timber is a magnet for red-headed woodpeckers and belted kingfishers noisily patrol the shallows. Painted turtles bask on logs that jut from the ponds while herons, egrets and bitterns stalk the marshy areas.

Directions: From U.S. 63, between Moberly and Macon, turn west on Route T and drive 6.3 miles to College Mound. Proceed to the labeled parking areas (see map) for the dayhikes described below.

Routes:

Cedar Knob Trail (CKT). From Route F, southeast of the lake, turn north on Road 11. Drive 1.2 miles and turn right (north) toward the boat ramp. Proceed another .3 mile and park along the road (P1). A wide trail leads down through the forest, crosses two streams and then climbs to a hilltop cedar glade which offers a view of the reservoir. This roundtrip hike is approximately 1.5 miles.

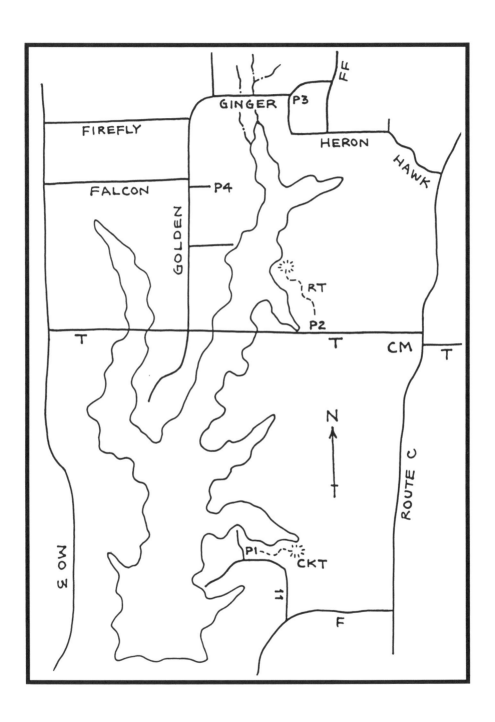

FIREFLY

GINGER   P3   FF

HERON

HAWK

FALCON   P4

GOLDEN

RT

P2

T   T   CM   T

N

MO 3

ROUTE C

P1   CKT

11

F

23

Ridge Trail (RT). From College Mound, drive west on Route T. Proceed 2 miles to a small lot (P2) on the right (north) side of the road. A trail leads to the north-northwest, climbing above an inlet of the lake and crossing open woodlands and meadows. The route eventually ends in a large field atop the ridge. This hike is approximately 2 miles roundtrip.

Ginger St. Hike. From Route C, 2.5 miles north of College Mound, turn west on Hawk Ave. Continue westward on Heron Ave.; bypass the FF junction, staying on the gravel road for another mile until you intersect Ginger Street (see map). Park at this intersection (P3) and hike westward on Ginger Street. This dirt-gravel road can be traversed by jeeps and trucks but is often impassable, especially in early spring. A half-mile hike will take you down to a backwater wetland of beaver ponds and bottomland forest. Several beaver dams are visible from the road and naturalists will find a tremendous variety of songbirds and amphibians here. Return to your car for a total roundtrip hike of 1 mile.

Northwest Loop (NWL). From College Mound, drive westward on Route T. Proceed 3.5 miles and turn north on Golden Ave. Drive another 1.9 miles and turn right on a gravel road which leads back to a parking lot (P4). Hike eastward from the lot, descending toward the lake on a wide path. Bear right at the trail junction and then turn left for a short walk along a field and thence through a narrow band of trees to the lakeshore. This is perhaps the best place at Thomas Hill Reservoir to scan the backwater shallows and to observe migrant shorebirds. If conditions permit, you can even take a stroll along the water's edge.

Return to the main trail loop, turn left and ascend from the lake basin. The trail skirts upland fields and meadows as it circles back to the parking area.

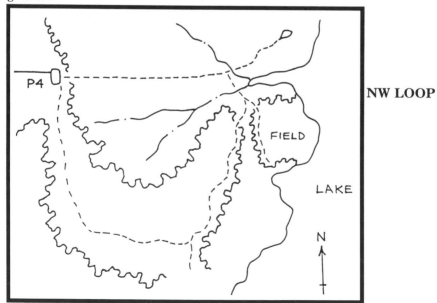

P4   NW LOOP   FIELD   LAKE   N

A beaver dam along Ginger Street

One of many streams that feed the reservoir

8 RUDOLF BENNITT CONSERVATION AREA

DISTANCE: DAYHIKES OF 1-2 MILES
TERRAIN: ROLLING TO HILLY
DIFFICULTY: EASY TO MODERATE
WALKING TIME: 1-1.5 HRS.

Located at the junction of Boone, Howard and Randolph Counties, the **Rudolf Bennitt Conservation Area** is bounded by Perche Creek (to the east) and Moniteau Creek (to the west). Its 3515 acres are characterized by a rolling terrain of forest, open woodlands and meadows; a relatively new lake also graces the preserve.

Numerous trails course through the area, most of which are open to horseback riding. As a result, some of the lowlands and stream crossings may become boggy during spring and early summer.

Directions: From U.S. 63, 20 miles north of Columbia (14 miles south of Moberly), turn west on Route F. Drive 5 miles and turn north on Route T. Proceed another 3.2 miles to the Area's main access road; a cemetery (C) is located at this intersection. Dayhikes that we recommend begin at lots P1-P6 (see map).

Routes: The following dayhikes are rather short. However, many of them can be combined by using portions of the graveled roadways that run through the preserve. Please note that trail names are purely descriptive and were created for the purposes of this guide.

Little Perche Creek Trail (LPC). This short hike (1 mile roundtrip) begins at lot P1 off Route T. The trail leads northward from the lot and then curves to the west, descending to the banks of Little Perche Creek. Return to your car via the same trail.

North Loop (NL). This 2 mile loop begins and ends at lot P2 on the main access road. The trail cuts northward across a meadow, curves to the west and then descends to cross a creek. Climbing onto the north wall of the valley, the route snakes westward and then southward, recrossing the stream near its upper end. Beyond the creek, the trail climbs to the roadway; turn left (east) and hike .7 mile back to the lot.

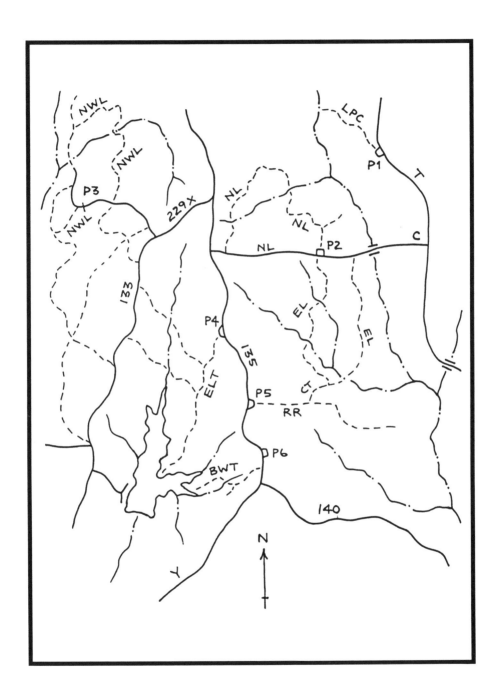

27

East Loop (EL). This 1.8 mile loop also begins and ends at lot P2. Cross the road and hike southward, descending into a valley, crossing the primary stream channel and then climbing onto the opposite wall. At the trail intersection, turn left. The path descends back to the creek, crosses it and climbs northward to the roadway. Turn left and walk a short distance back to the parking lot.

This hike may be lengthened by using the **Connector Trail (CT)** which leads to the Ridge Road (RR).

Northwest Loop (NWL). This loop begins at lot P3 above the Moniteau Creek valley. Hike southwestward on the gated roadway, continuing straight ahead on a trail that descends into the floodplain. At the intersection, turn right, heading upstream. Bear left at the roadway, cross the stream and hike a short distance before turning right (east) into the forest. The route undulates through this woodland, recrossing the creek and then climbing to the roadway. Turn right on the road and return to your car. This 2 mile loop is moderately difficult due to the hilly terrain.

East Lake Trail (ELT). A pulloff (P4) along Road 135 services this trail which leads through forest and open woodlands to the east shore of the Area's lake. The terrain is flat to gently rolling and the route follows a wide jeep path; in addition, horses are not permitted on this trail. All of these factors, combined with a scenic destination, make for a pleasant dayhike. The roundtrip distance is 1.8 miles.

Ridge Road (RR). This old, graveled roadway, now closed to traffic, begins at a small lot (P5) on the east side of Road 135 (see map). The road follows high ground between two drainages and offers a pleasant stroll through the forest; roundtrip distance from the roadway is approximately 2 miles. As mentioned above, this trail can be combined with the East Loop (EL) by using the **Connector Trail (CT)**.

Backwater Trail (BWT). A short hike (1.6 miles roundtrip) to the lake's eastern backwaters begins at lot P6 on Road 135. Walk southward on the roadway for .1 mile and pick up a trail that leads westward along the edge of a meadow. Turn right at the trail intersection, descending into the lake basin. Cross a stream and walk down to the water's edge. Wood ducks and belted kingfishers are often found in this backwater habitat. Return to your car via the same route.

Wildflowers paint a meadow at Rudolf Bennitt

An autumn scene along the lake's backwaters

29

9 MARK TWAIN LAKE & VICINITY

DISTANCE: DAYHIKES OF 1 TO 20 MILES
TERRAIN: ROLLING TO HILLY
DIFFICULTY: EASY TO MODERATE
WALKING TIME: 1 TO 14 HRS.

While most of the streams of Central Missouri flow toward the Missouri River, the northeast region is drained by the Salt River and its tributaries which flow eastward to join the Mississippi. The Salt River has carved a broad valley in the Glaciated Plains of Monroe and Ralls Counties which, today, holds **Mark Twain Lake**, an 18,000 acre multipurpose reservoir. Construction of the **Clarence Cannon Dam** was authorized by Congress in 1962, part of the Flood Control Act; the reservoir also provides regional hydroelectric power, augments local water supplies, offers recreational opportunities and creates habitat for migrant and nesting waterfowl.

The Lake is surrounded by numerous Recreation Areas and is home to Mark Twain State Park; hiking trails are currently limited to the State Park, to the Lick Creek corridor and to lands bordering the northeast shore.

Directions: Hiking areas are best reached from Missouri 154 which runs along the south edge of the reservoir basin and from Route J, which leads northward from Perry and crosses the Clarence Cannon Dam.

The trails of **Mark Twain State Park** are accessed from the Campground Road and the Buzzard's Roost Picnic Area on the west side of Missouri 107, less than a mile north of Missouri 154 (see map).

The **Lick Creek Trail** can be entered from trailheads on the east side of Route J; these include the Duane Wheelan Recreation Area (2.7 miles north of Perry), Hunter Access Site 62 (3.6 miles north of Perry) and the Main Trailhead, (8 miles north of Perry).

The **Ray Behrens Recreation Area**, site of the **Hickory Bluff Trail**, is on the west side of Route J, 8 miles north of Perry.

To reach the **Joanna Trail**, proceed northward from the Clarence Cannon Dam on Route J. Drive approximately 3 miles and turn left (west) on Landing Lane. Proceed 1 mile to Oakland Rd. and turn left (south). Enter the John F. Spalding Recreation Area and bear right (toward the boat ramp); the parking lot for the Joanna Trail will be a short distance ahead, on your left.

A **North Shore Trail** (our terminology) runs from Hunter Site 11 (at the south end of Route N) through Hunter Site 10 and on to the Joanna Trail. Route N leads southward from U.S. 24, approximately 3.5 miles southwest of Monroe City. For access to Hunter Site 10, see the overview map.

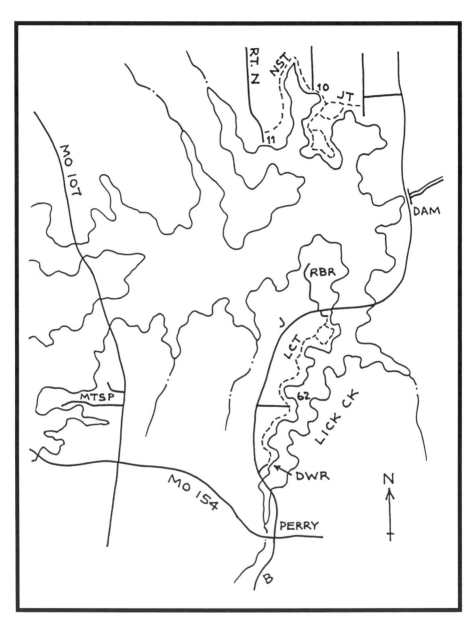

MARK TWAIN LAKE: OVERVIEW MAP

Routes: The trails of the Mark Twain Lake region will be presented in the following groups: Mark Twain State Park, the Lick Creek Trail, the Ray Behrens Recreation Area and the Joanna/North Shore Trails.

MARK TWAIN STATE PARK

A network of interconnecting trail loops lead westward from Missouri 107, a short distance north of Missouri 154. Dayhikers should park at the **Buzzard's Roost Picnic Area** (see map). Due to the hilly terrain, these trails are of moderate difficulty; a combined hike, described below, covers a distance of 5.5 miles.

Pick up the **Whitetail Trail (WT)**, a .5 mile loop, southwest of the Overlook. Bear right at the junction, hiking above Mark Twain Lake and soon turning southward above an inlet. Pick up the **Dogwood Trail (DT)**, which continues southward, and bear right onto this 2.5 mile loop; the trail crosses several streams, curves back to the northwest and winds above the reservoir once again.

Bear right at the next intersection, circling above another inlet and soon connecting with the north arm of the **Post Oak Trail (PT)**, a 2 mile loop. Stay right (north) on this loop for another excursion above Mark Twain Lake before winding southward to cross several drainages. A final curve to the south brings you to an intersection with the **White Oak Trail (WO)**; this 1 mile loop leads further west onto a peninsula between arms of the reservoir (see map).

Complete this loop and rejoin the **Post Oak Trail**, following its south arm as it crosses the boat ramp road and winds above a scenic arm of the South Fork. This trail eventually descends toward the lakeshore and then leads eastward along a feeder stream. Bear right at the next intersection, crossing and recrossing the main creek before reaching the west end of the **Dogwood Trail** loop (see map). Since the south arm of this loop is currently under development, turn left (north) and hike up to the Campground Road. Turn right (east) on the road and walk to the east end of the Dogwood Trail loop. Hike northward on this trail, switch to the **Whitetail Trail** and return to the Buzzard's Roost Picnic Area.

A view from the Dogwood Trail

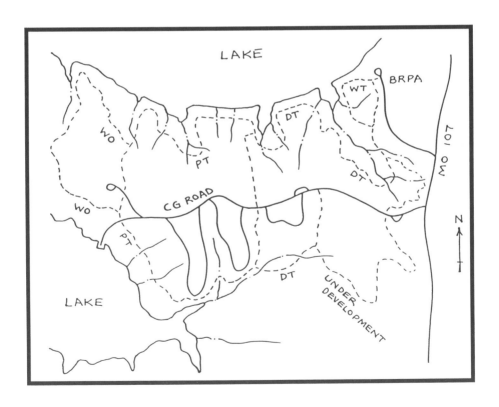

The **Lick Creek Trail**, maintained by the Youngblood Saddle Club, is an eight mile path which follows the course of the Lake's Lick Creek arm, from the Duane Wheelan Recreation Area to the Ray Behren's Recreation Area. The best access point is at the **Main Trailhead**, at the north end of the trail (see map). The trail is a popular route for horseback riders but, due to the rocky soil, footing is generally good and hikers will find few boggy areas.

Unless two vehicles are used, the entire 16-mile roundtrip distance is a bit long for a dayhike. Those who start at the Main Trailhead may want to set their sites on **Hunter Access Lot 62** (see overview map); this destination is five miles from the trailhead, yielding a 10-mile roundtrip hike. Those desiring a shorter hike can use the **Short Loop**, illustrated on page 35. From the Main Trailhead, the Lick Creek Trail leads to the southwest, crossing two creeks and then climbing to a trail intersection. Bear left onto the Short Loop which snakes out to a backcountry campsite above the Lick Creek arm of Mark Twain Lake. The trail then curves westward above the lake, yielding broad views to the south, and eventually intersects the Main Trail. Turn right, passing a woodland pond, and return to the trailhead lot. This Short Loop yields a 2-mile dayhike.

Mark Twain Lake

A view from the point: Short Loop Trail

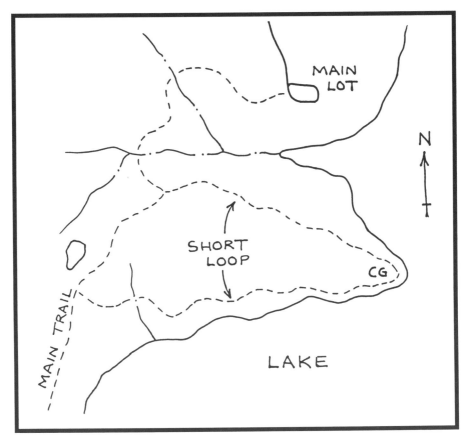

SHORT LOOP, LICK CREEK TRAIL

The **Ray Behrens Recreation Area** is on the south shore of Mark Twain Lake, just west of the Lick Creek arm. It is accessed from Route J, approximately 8 miles north of Perry. The Area is closed from the onset of deer season, in November, until mid March.

A **Nature Trail (NT)**, approximately 2 miles in total length, connects the campground areas and the Park's Amphitheater (A); this trail is easily combined with the **Hickory Bluff Trail (HBT)** which starts on the west side of the main roadway (see map).

The **Hickory Bluff Trail** leads westward through a cedar grove and soon reaches an intersection. Turn right for a short hike onto a rocky ridge which overlooks an inlet of Mark Twain Lake. Return to the intersection and continue straight ahead, crossing the east wall of a stream valley. At the next junction, turn right and descend to the creek. The trail crosses the main channel and then climbs westward along a tributary before splitting into a loop (see map). Hike either direction, skirting cropfields and a ridgetop meadow before arriving at a pond-side wildlife blind. Complete the loop, descend and ascend through the creek valley and, at the junction, continue straight ahead to the park roadway. The Hickory Bluff Trail covers a total distance of 2 miles.

Winter woods along the Hickory Bluff Trail

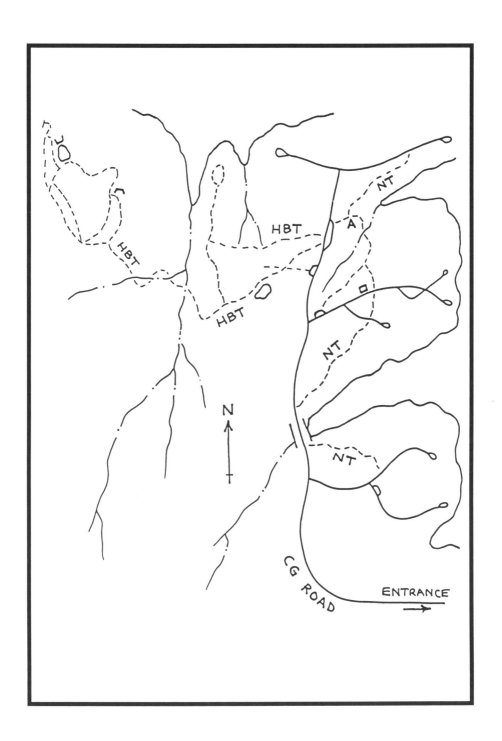

JOANNA TRAIL/NORTH SHORE TRAIL

Maintained by the Monroe County Saddle Club, the **Joanna Trail** yields two potential dayhikes along and near the north shore of Mark Twain Lake. Both are accessed from a lot at the John F. Spalding Recreation Area (see Directions for this Chapter). The trail is blazed with yellow paint and metal markers; a few of the larger stream crossings may be impassable when the lake level is high.

The **Short Loop (SL)** covers 5.5 miles while the **Long Loop (LL)** yields an 11 mile excursion. Both cross a mix of forest and meadow, offering views of the lake along the way. The Short Loop offers a reasonable goal for dayhikers and we thus limited our research to this segment; cutoffs to the Long Loop are shown on the map. To complete the **Short Loop**, hike westward from the trailhead, entering the forest and undulating across several drainages. The trail soon curves to the north to cross an inlet area; these larger creek valleys may be impassable during periods of wet weather. Climbing back into the forest, the path splits; bear left, hiking above the inlet and then following the edge of a large meadow.

Back in the woods, the trail snakes westward and southward, crossing several small streams and eventually passing a woodland pond. A short distance beyond this pond, the path skirts the edge of a large field and reaches a trail junction. Turn right, hiking northward and following the west edge of the field. Bypass a cutoff to the Long Loop, on your left and you will soon reach another intersection where a trail leads westward toward Hunter Access Lot 11 (this is the North Shore Trail, described below). Continue northward and then eastward, passing the original trail junction and returning the the Spalding Recreation Area (see map).

The Joanna Trail also provides access to the **North Shore Trail (NST;** our terminology) which parallels the shoreline of Mark Twain Lake from Hunter Access Lot 11, at the south end of Route N, to the northwest side of the Joanna Trail loop. Along the way, it passes through Hunter Access Lot 10 (see overview map); this lot is approximately 2 miles from the Joanna Trail junction. The entire North Shore Trail covers a distance of 10 miles (20 miles roundtrip).

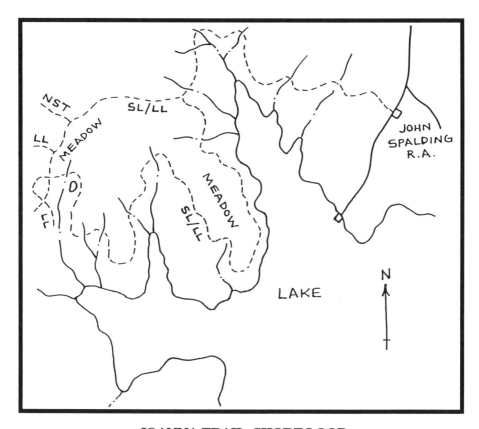

JOANNA TRAIL: SHORT LOOP

10 ROBERT M. WHITE II CONSERVATION AREA

DISTANCE: DAYHIKES OF 1-2 MILES
TERRAIN: FLAT TO ROLLING
DIFFICULTY: EASY
WALKING TIME: 1-1.5 HRS.

There is nothing special about the **Robert M. White II Conservation Area**, north of Mexico. No scenic gorges, ridgetop bluffs or natural bridges grace the preserve and the rolling landscape is typical of much of northern Missouri. Yet, this 1163 acre refuge, donated to the State by Mr. White, a dedicated conservationist, offers a peaceful escape for the city dweller and entices the naturalist with a fine diversity of habitat. A fifteen acre lake and numerous ponds dot the preserve and Young's Creek, a tributary of the Salt River's South Fork, bisects the refuge.

Directions: From Mexico, drive north on Missouri 15. Proceed 8.2 miles and turn right (east) on Route Z. Drive another 1.7 miles to the junction with Route ZZ; to reach the south lot, turn right on ZZ and proceed 1.9 miles to the access road. Those heading to the north lot should stay on Route Z for another 2.3 miles and then turn right on Road 386; drive 1 mile and turn right on Road 390 which leads back to the parking lot.

Routes: Hikers will find two primary trails at this Conservation Area. The **South Trail** (our terminology) is of most interest, passing the preserve's large lake and ending at a secluded pond (see map). The trail passes many natural borders, where woodlands meet meadow or where wetlands blend with forest; such areas attract a variety of wildlife species, from songbirds to raccoons. Barn and tree swallows swoop above the lake during the warmer months and herons often stalk the shallows. Red-tailed hawks and turkey vultures patrol the meadows, replaced by great horned owls as dusk envelops the refuge. A westward extension of this trail leads up through an open meadow to an old barn (B); northern bobwhites are abundant in this area and late-day visitors may spot a red fox hunting on the fields. The South Trail is approximately 1 mile in length (2 miles roundtrip).

The **North Trail** heads eastward as a gravel road, following an open corridor in the forest. A side trail leads down to a field in the Young's Creek Valley while the main trail continues eastward to an upland crop field; the gravel ends here and the path follows the south edge of the field before entering the forest at its east edge. The trail leads through the woodland before ending at another field (see map). The roundtrip hike on the North Trail covers a distance of 2 miles.

Meadows and open woodlands cloak the preserve

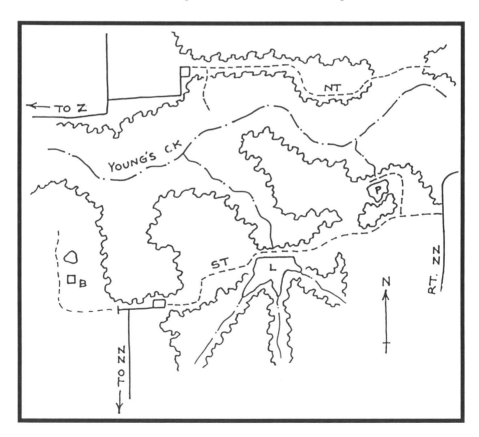

11 FRANKLIN ISLAND CONSERVATION AREA

DISTANCE: DAYHIKES OF 2-6.8 MILES
TERRAIN: FLAT
DIFFICULTY: EASY
WALKING TIME: 1.5-4 HRS.

Characterized by meadows, floodplain woodlands and crop fields, the 1625 acres of the **Franklin Island Conservation Area** are bounded by Bonne Femme Creek and the Missouri River. Infact, the land of this refuge was actually an island in the Missouri River until 1952 when the River's north channel was cut off by construction of a levee.

Gravel roads and a network of levees provide access to the preserve which is home to white-tailed deer, wild turkeys and an excellent variety of birdlife. Bald eagles visit the area in winter and both red-tailed hawks and northern harriers are commonly seen here. Migrants include waterfowl, shorebirds, ospreys and terns. Flooded woodlands attract red-headed woodpeckers while meadowlarks, bluebirds and a variety of sparrows forage on the grasslands. By allowing forest to invade the adjacent fields and by planting groves of native trees, refuge managers hope to convert Franklin Island back to its original state, a rich floodplain woodland.

Directions: Franklin Island Conservation Area is accessed from the south side of U.S. 40, approximately 2 miles northeast of Boonville.

Routes: The graveled roads and levees of this Conservation Area permit a variety of dayhike routes. Parking areas and sectional mileages are noted on the map. Hikers can thus choose a route based upon time allotment and their level of conditioning.

Levees provide access to this floodplain refuge

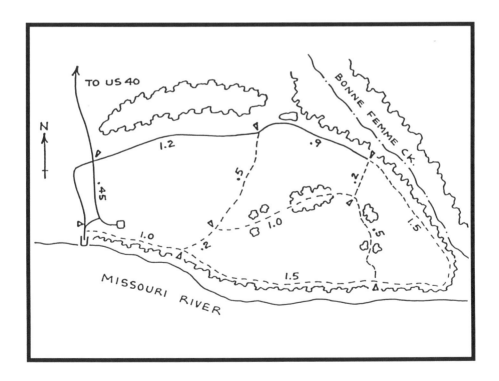

12 DAVISDALE CONSERVATION AREA

SOUTH LOOP
  DISTANCE: 6.5 MILES
  TERRAIN: HILLY
  DIFFICULTY: MODERATE
  WALKING TIME: 4 HRS.

RIDGE TRAIL
  DISTANCE: 3..5 MILES RT
  TERRAIN: ROLLING
  DIFFICULTY: EASY
  WALKING TIME: 2 HRS.

NORTHWEST LOOP
  DISTANCE: 2 MILES
  TERRAIN: HILLY
  DIFFICULTY: MODERATE
  WALKING TIME: 1.5 HRS.

NORTHEAST LOOP
  DISTANCE: 2.5 MILES
  TERRAIN: HILLY
  DIFFICULTY: MODERATE
  WALKING TIME: 1.75 HRS.

The rolling terrain of the **Davisdale Conservation Area** sits atop the north wall of the Missouri River Valley. A composite of old farmlands, the area was the birthplace of General Omar Bradley. Today, the refuge attracts hunters and naturalists with an appealing mix of woodlands, meadows, crop fields and wetlands. Access to this 2701 acre preserve is provided by a network of gravel road and field trails.

Directions: From I-70, take Exit 121 and head west on U.S. 40. The junction with Missouri 240 will be 8.8 miles ahead; the junction with the 240 cutoff will be 9.8 miles; the access road to lot P1 will be 11.4 miles.
To reach lots P2 and P3 from U.S 40, turn right (north) on the 240 cutoff, proceed .5 mile and turn left (west) on 442; lot P2 will be 1.25 miles ahead and lot P3 will be 2.75 miles.
To reach lot P4 from U.S. 40, turn right (north) on Missouri 240 and proceed 3.6 miles to 449; turn left on 449 and drive another .5 mile to the lot.

Routes: We suggest the following dayhikes; the trail names are purely descriptive.
  South Loop (SL). This 6.5 mile loop begins and ends at lot P1, just north of U.S. 40, which also services the Katy Trail (see Chapter 26). Hike northward, crossing the Katy Trail and a stream. Passing an old homestead, the trail climbs rather steeply onto the ridge. Bear left at the trail junction, curving west and soon enjoying broad views of the Missouri River Valley. Continuing westward, the trail descends into a valley and then turns north, crossing the creek and beginning a long, steady climb to Road 442.
Cut through lot P3, cross the road and angle to the northeast. At the trail junction, pick up the Ridge Trail (RT) which leads across open country and snakes northeastward. Within a half mile or so you will reach another trail junction. Bear right, picking up the east arm of the South Loop (see map) which gradually curves to the southeast and begins a long

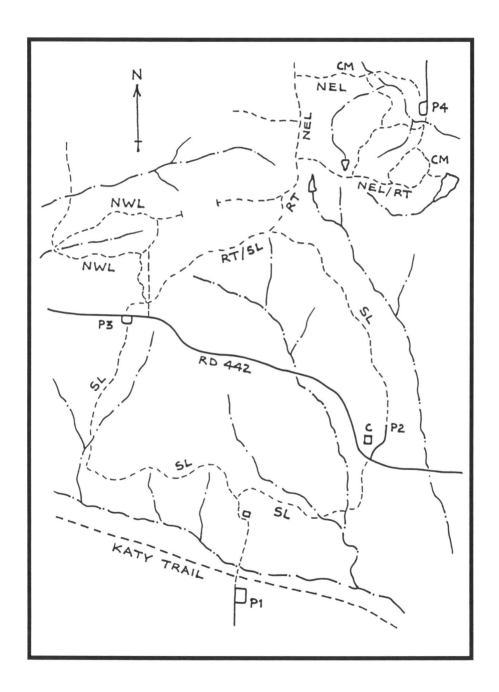

descent to Road 442, where parking area P2 sits next to a church and cemtery.

Cross the road, continuing southward through forest and open woods. The trail eventually curves to the west, crosses the main creek and a tributary and soon re-connects with your entry route. Turn left and walk down to lot P1.

Ridge Trail (RT). This pleasant, 1.75 mile trail (3.5 miles roundtrip) begins at lot P3 on Road 442 (see map). Hike northeastward to the trail junction and then continue to the northeast on the Ridge Trail which follows high ground across open country and yields broad views along the way. Bear left at the junction with the South Loop and then right at the next two intersections (see map). Heading east, the Ridge Trail joins the south arm of the Northeast Loop (NEL) before descending to the refuge's largest lake. After rest and refreshment at the lake, return to lot P3 via the same route, completing a roundtrip hike of 3.5 miles.

Northwest Loop (NWL). This 2 mile loop begins and ends at lot P3 on Road 442. Cross the road and hike northeastward to the trail junction; bear left here, undulating northward at the edge of a wooded meadow. Bear left again at the next junction, soon descending to a stream crossing; after crossing the creek, turn right for a long, gradual climb to the east. Leveling out atop the ridge, the path reaches another intersection; turn right, walk a short distance and then bear left, hiking back to Road 442 and lot P3 (see map).

Northeast Loop (NEL). This 2.5 mile loop begins and ends at lot P4 on Road 449. From the lot, hike northwestward across a field, soon crossing a stream. Continue straight ahead at the trail junction, beginning a long, steady climb to the west across an open ridge. At the crest of this ridge you will pass an old cemetery (CM) with graves dating from the mid 1800s. Hike westward to a trail intersection and turn left (south). Bypass a cutoff on your right and proceed to the junction with the Ridge Trail (RT); turn left (east) here and take either cutoff on your left to return to lot P4 (see map). You may want to take the second cutoff which leads past another 19th Century cemetery (CM).

*Old farm ponds, meadows and open woodlands
characterize this preserve*

A wooded stream near the southern trailhead

13 ROCKY FORK LAKES
CONSERVATION AREA

SOUTH TRAIL
  DISTANCE: 3 MILES RT
  TERRAIN: FLAT
  DIFFICULTY: EASY
  WALKING TIME: 2 HRS.

NORTH LOOP
  DISTANCE: 2.3 MILES
  TERRAIN: ROLLING
  DIFFICULTY: MODERATE
  WALKING TIME: 1.5 HRS.

SOUTH LAKE TRAIL
  DISTANCE: 3 MIILES RT
  TERRAIN: ROLLING, FEW HILLS
  DIFFICULTY: EASY
  WALKING TIME: 2 HRS.

Formerly a strip mine, owned and operated by the Peabody Coal Co., **Rocky Fork Lakes Conservation Area**, six miles north of Columbia, was purchased by the State of Missouri in 1979. Covering 2200 acres, the preserve is characterized by a central lake, wooded ponds, fields, open woodlands and parcels of forest. Access is via a network of gravel roads and jeep trails. Seasonal hunting is permitted here but, for much of the year, Rocky Fork is an excellent destination for hiking, birdwatching and nature study.

Directions: The road to Finger Lakes State Park and Rocky Fork Lakes Conservation Area leads east from U.S. 63, 9.2 miles north of I-70. Proceed 1 mile, bypassing the State Park entrance and enter the Conservation Area. Park in one of the lots (P1, P2) illustrated on the map.

Routes: The names used for the following trails are purely descriptive.
  South Trail (ST). From lot P1, hike southward on the gravel road. Bypass the first two cutoffs (see map), curving southeastward at a pond and staying on the roadbed. This scenic route passes marshes, open forest, wooded ponds and meadows. A 1.5 mile hike brings you to a small pond with a broad, deep basin. Just beyond this site you will reach an intersection where the coal mine's old railroad bed crosses the trail. The Area's boundary is just beyond this intersection. Return to your car via the same route for a roundtrip hike of 3.0 miles.

  South Lake Trail (SLT). While the official Conservation Area map suggests that a loop hike can be achieved south of the Lake, part of this loop is currently overgrown and very difficult to follow. We thus recommend the following "out and back" hike which yields a roundtrip distance of 3 miles.
  From lot P1, hike southward on the gravel road and take the first cutoff

A scene along the South Trail

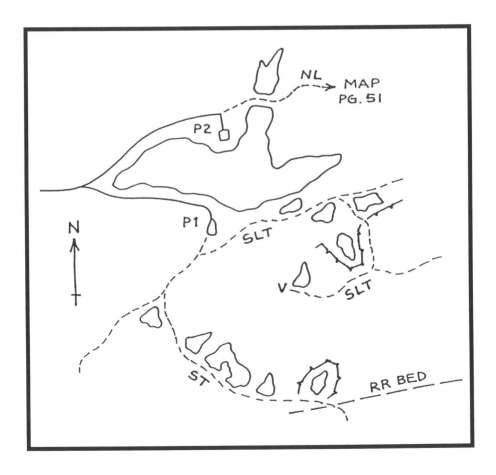

on your left. This jeep trail climbs toward the east, passing through open woodlands. The trail forks at a large pond; bear right on the primary route, climbing gradually to the southeast and skirting another pond, on your left.

The trail soon negotiates a rock escarpment via a short, rocky slope and then winds southward above the chasm. Bypass a faint cutoff on your left and continue to the next trail junction. Turn right, crossing an open, grassy ridge. Re-entering the woodland, the route dips toward a rock-lined pond and then ascends to a point which offers a magnificent view (V) to the north and west. Beyond this point the trail is overgrown and difficult to follow; we thus recommend that you turn back here and follow the same route back to lot P1.

North Loop (NL). Adventurous hikers may want to try this scenic, 2.3 mile loop north of the lake; much of the route is overgrown during the summer months and close attention to the narrative and map is recommended.

From lot P2, pick up the gravel road that leads eastward, crossing the lake's north inlet. A large marsh at this inlet attracts a wide variety of wetland birds. The road climbs above the east edge of the inlet and then descends to a basin with two ponds; bypass the grassy cutoff on your right. Bear left at the trail junction, skirting the edge of a pond and then climbing onto an open ridge which parallels a rock outcropping. Beyond the east end of this outcrop the trail turn southward and re-enters the woodland. Bypass a faint trail crossing and continue straight ahead (eastward) through the forest. After passing a large meadow, on your left, the trail curves to the south once again.

Running along the edge of the preserve, the route descends through a cedar glade and then angles to the west. Cross a creekbed and climb onto a low ridge, passing another pond on your left. Within a short distance you are treated to a fine view (V) to the northwest. Continue westward atop this low ridge, crossing a small meadow and then entering a large clearing. The trail climbs northward through this open grassland, passing scenic ponds, and then turns to the west at the top of the ridge. After skirting a rock-walled pond, the trail crosses its outlet stream and descends to the trail junction. Bear left and return to lot P2.

Old quarry ponds dot the woodland

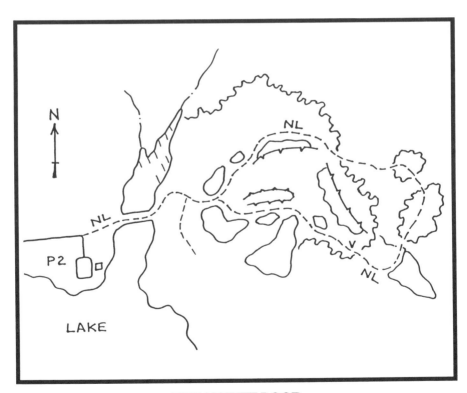

THE NORTH LOOP

14 WHETSTONE CREEK CONSERVATION AREA

DISTANCE: DAYHIKES OF 1-5.5 MILES
TERRAIN: FLAT TO ROLLING
DIFFICULTY: EASY
WALKING TIME: 1-3 HRS.

Whetstone Creek, a major tributary of the Loutre River, flows eastward through northern Callaway County. A four-mile stretch of its valley and adjacent uplands have been set aside as the **Whetstone Creek Conservation Area**. This 5147 acre preserve, known locally as "The Ranch," is accessed by gravel jeep roads and grassy field trails, appealing avenues for hiking and nature study. White-tailed deer are often spotted on the meadows and the open country of this refuge is a good place for watching hawks, kestrels and vultures. Wildflowers can be spectacular here in spring and late summer.

Directions: From I-70, take the Williamsburg Exit (#161). Turn north on Route D which soon angles to the west. Proceed .9 mile and turn right (north) on Road 1003. The Conservation Area will be 1 mile ahead; the best hiking opportunities originate at lot P1 (see map).

Routes: A number of potential dayhikes are possible at the Whetstone Creek Conservation Area. We suggest the following routes.

Whetstone Creek from lot P1. A gravel road leads northward from lot P1, crossing open country. Within a half mile it intersects cutoffs on either side; continue straight ahead, eventually descending to the creek. The roundtrip hike from P1 to Whetstone Creek is 3 miles.

Lot P1 to Route EE. Hike northward from lot P1 to Whetstone Creek as described above. The gravel road crosses the creek, angles to the northwest, fords a sidestream and climbs onto the north wall of the valley. Leaving the woodlands, the road winds across open country to Route EE. The roundtrip hike from P1 to Route EE is approximately 5.5 miles.

Lot P1 to lot P2 (on Road 1005). Hike northward from P1 and, within .5 mile, turn right (east) on a gravel jeep road which soon enters an open woodland and begins a gradual descent to lot P2. An small pond is just south of the trail near its junction with Road 1005 (see map). The roundtrip hike from lot P1 to lot P2 is approximately 3 miles.

Lot P3 to Whetstone Creek. Those desiring a shorter hike to Whetstone Creek can start at lot P3 (see map). A gravel jeep road leads northwestward from the lot while a field trail heads to the northeast. The roundtrip hike to Whetstone Creek is 1 mile via the gravel road and 1.5 miles via the field trail.

A foggy morning on Whetstone Creek

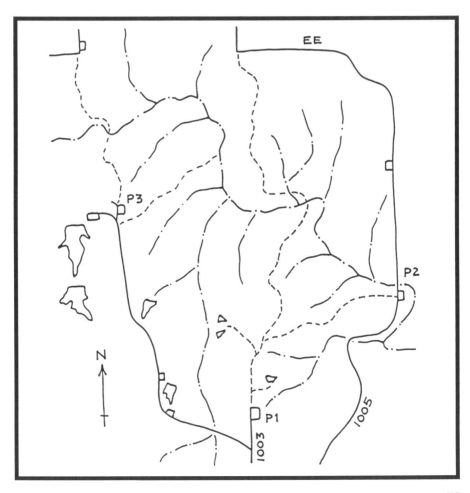

15 GRAHAM CAVE STATE PARK

DISTANCE: DAYHIKES OF .75 TO 4.25 MILES
TERRAIN: ROLLING TO HILLY
DIFFICULTY: EASY TO MODERATE
WALKING TIME: .5 TO 2.5 HRS.

A site of refuge and inspiration for over 10,000 years, **Graham Cave** is now the centerpiece of a Missouri State Park. The 100 foot recessed cave, hollowed from an outcropping of St. Peter sandstone (Ordovician age), is named for Dr. Robert Graham who purchased the cave property in 1816 from Daniel Boone's son. Today, the cave is undergoing study by University of Missouri archaeologists and is thus closed to the public.

Graham Cave State Park covers 356 acres along the east wall of the Loutre River valley. Three trails, described below, provide off-road access for hikers and naturalists.

Directions: From I-70, take Exit 170 and proceed to the north side of the highway. Turn west on Route TT (a frontage road) and drive 2 miles to the State Park. Parking lots are illustrated on the map.

Routes:
Graham Cave Loop (GCL). This .75 mile loop begins and ends at the cave access lot (P1). Hike north on a paved trail to the base of Graham Cave. The trail continues east of the cave, descending to cross a sidestream and then winding up the valley of the primary creek. Curving southward, the path crosses the creek and soon hugs the south wall of the valley, passing a wall of sandstone. It then angles to the west and returns to lot P1.

Indian Glade Trail (IGT). This 1 mile trail (2 miles roundtrip) connects the Graham Cave area with the Park's Campground. The trail leaves the west side of Graham Cave, enters the forest and climbs to the Park's central roadway. After crossing the road, the trail makes a broad curve toward the north where it intersects a secondary path that leads in from the picnic area (see map). The main trail continues northwestward, snaking through the woodland and crossing two creeks before reaching the campground road.

Loutre River Trail (LRT). This 1.5 mile loop begins just south of the campground restrooms. Heading southward, the trail parallels the campground road before turning to the southwest and descending to the Loutre River. The primary loop trail follows the river upstream; bypass the connector trail (CT) and continue on the main route as it climbs northward along a tributary and returns to the campground road.

Combined Route. By combining the above trails, energetic hikers will cover a distance of 4.25 miles.

54

Graham Cave

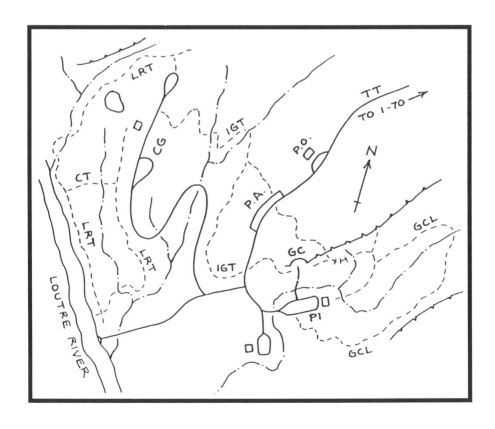

16 DANVILLE CONSERVATION AREA

EAST LOOP HIKE
  DISTANCE: 3-5 MILES
  TERRAIN: HILLY
  DIFFICULTY: MODERATE
  WALKING TIME: 2-3.5 HRS.

NATURE TRAIL
  DISTANCE: 3-4 MILES
  TERRAIN: HILLY
  DIFFICULTY: MODERATE
  WALKING TIME: 2-2.5 HRS.

The **Danville Conservation Area** covers 2654 acres in east-central Missouri. Characterized by ridgetop meadows and forested ravines, the refuge is also known for its glade communities, most of which are clustered in the northwest section of the preserve. In these areas, thin, dry soil overlies the limestone bedrock, creating conditions that are more typical of the western U.S. As a result, one can find western flora such as Indian paintbrush, coneflowers and shrubby St. John's-wort in these glades.

The Conservation Area is also home to an excellent variety of wildlife, including white-tailed deer, wild turkey, raccoons and coyotes. Hikers should be aware that rattlesnakes and copperheads also inhabit this refuge; these dangerous reptiles are best avoided by staying on designated trails.

Directions: From I-70, take the Danville Exit (#170). Proceed to the south side of the highway and turn east on the frontage road. Drive 2.2 miles to Route RB. Turn right (south) on RB and drive another 2.7 miles to the junction with Turkey Ridge Road (see map); proceed to the parking lots, as illustrated.

Routes: While there are a number of potential dayhikes at the Danville Conservation Area, we suggest the following routes.

East Loop Hike (EL). A 3 mile loop begins and ends at lot P1; energetic hikers may want to start at lot P2, thereby increasing the total distance to 5 miles. From lot P2, a trail leads southward across an upland meadow, eventually crossing through a gate and turning eastward. It then enters the forest and descends to the valley floor. Turn left at the trail intersection and hike northward to lot P1, bypassing an arm of the East Loop along the way (see map). Just north of the parking lot, the trail crosses the creek and continues upstream along the valley floor. After crossing under the powerlines the path begins to climb away from the stream, soon passing a series of rocky overlooks. It then turns eastward for a final climb to the ridgetop meadow. Turn right at the trail intersection, hiking southward through the meadow and passing two small ponds along the way. The trail eventually curves to the west, re-enters the forest and descends back to the valley floor. Turn left at the junction and then take a right on the path that leads back to lot P2 (see map).

56

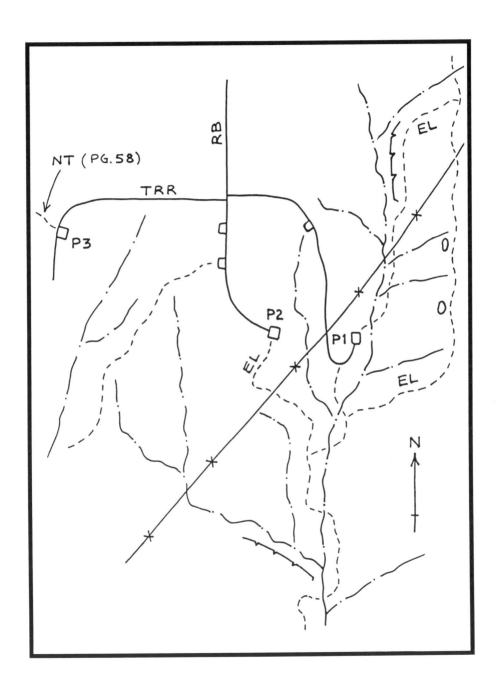

NT (PG.58)

The **Nature Trail (NT)**. The preserve's nature trail begins across Turkey Ridge Road from lot P3 (see map). After crossing a meadow, the trail enters the forest and descends into a valley. The path crosses a sidestream and the main creek channel before turning southward and climbing the west wall via a broad switchback. Leveling out atop the ridge, the trail leads northward via an old roadbed and eventually enters a large meadow.

Paralleling the west edge of this field, the Nature Trail leads up to an old farm pond. After circling this pond, the trail heads southward, re-enters the forest and then ends at a secluded meadow. Returning to lot P3 via this same route yields a roundtrip hike of 3 miles. Those wishing to lengthen the hike can take a side trail northward along the west edge of the large field, continuing out to a powerline swath at the northwest corner of the refuge. This clearing yields a broad view to the north and west.

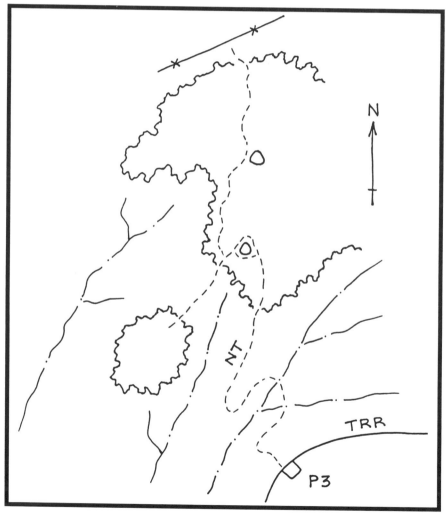

Winter on the East Loop

Crossing a ridgetop meadow

17 LITTLE DIXIE LAKE CONSERVATION AREA

WEST SHORE LOOP
  DISTANCE: 2.7 MILES
  TERRAIN: FLAT
  DIFFICULTY: EASY
  WALKING TIME: 2 HRS.

NORTHEAST LOOP
  DISTANCE: 2 MILES
  TERRAIN: ROLLING
  DIFFICULTY: MODERATE
  WALKING TIME: 1.5 HRS.

SOUTH SHORE HIKE
  DISTANCE: 2.5 MILES
  TERRAIN: FLAT
  DIFFICULTY: EASY
  WALKING TIME: 2 HRS.

LAKE LOOP
  DISTANCE: 5 MILES
  TERRAIN: ROLLING
  DIFFICULTY: MODERATE
  WALKING TIME: 3.5 HRS.

Little Dixie Lake, created by damming Owl Creek, is the centerpiece of this 733 acre Conservation Area, 10 miles east of Columbia. The 205 acre lake attracts an excellent variety of waterfowl during the spring and fall migration and is a winter sanctuary for geese and bald eagles. The refuge is thus a popular destination for bird watchers.

Hikers will find two primary trails at the preserve: the **Boundary Trail (BT)** and the **Shoreline Trail (ST)**. A paved interpretive trail, the **Dixie Woods Nature Trail (NT)**, is accessed via the east shore parking lot (P2). Open woodlands, meadows, crop fields, marsh-lined ponds and an oak-hickory forest characterize the refuge which is home to wild turkeys, pileated woodpeckers and white-tailed deer. Seasonal archery hunting is permitted across northern sections of the Conservation Area.

Directions: From U.S. 63 on the east side of Columbia, take Route WW east. Drive 9.7 miles to the junction with Route J and proceed to parking areas as illustrated on the map.

Routes: By combining sections of the Boundary and Shoreline Trails, one can plan a variety of dayhikes. We suggest the following routes.

West Shore Loop. This 2.7 mile loop hike begins and ends at the southwest parking lot (P1). Hike northward on the **Shoreline Trail (ST)**; this path winds in and out of the lakeside woodlands and offers broad views of Little Dixie Lake along the way. Bypass cutoffs to the Boundary Trail (BT), continuing north to an open area where rocky piers jut into the lake; this area is just east of lot P3 (see map).

Return to your car via the **Boundary Trail**. We suggest bypassing a segment of this trail (between the two asterisks on the map), switching to the **Shoreline Trail** and thereby avoiding a residential area.

60

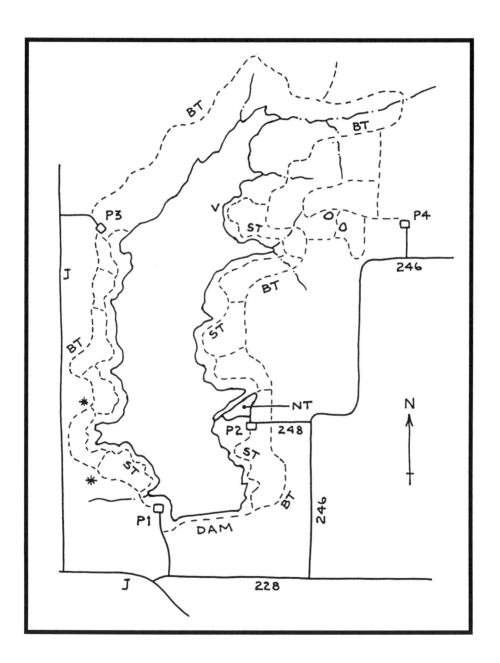

South Shore Hike. A roundtrip hike across the dam, combined with a loop on the **Dixie Woods Nature Trail (NT)**, yields a dayhike of 2.5 miles. Begin at lot P1, on the southwest shore of the lake, and pickup the **Shoreline Trail** via the entry road. Hike eastward atop the dam; loons, grebes, coot and diving ducks congregate on these deeper waters and ospreys fish on the lake during the spring and fall migrations.

Continue across the dam and then turn northward, winding along the lakeshore. Cross the east parking lot (P2) and stroll along the paved **Nature Trail** which provides lake access for disabled visitors. After completing the loop, return to your car via the same route.

Northeast Loop. Park in lot P4, north of Route 246 (see map). Hike to the west for a short distance and bear right (north) on a wide path that leads across an upland meadow and then descends toward a streambed. Turn left on the **Boundary Trail (BT)**, hiking through a boggy woodland and soon climbing into the drier lakeside forest. Curving southward, the path crosses several drainages; cut out to a lakeside **viewpoint (V)** and then loop back to the Boundary Trail via a section of the **Shoreline Trail**.

Turn left for a short distance and then turn right (see map), climbing into the forest. Bear left onto a trail that leads past several ponds before intersecting another trail; turn right (east) here and return to lot P4, completing a dayhike of 2 miles.

Lake Loop. A five-mile loop hike around Little Dixie Lake can be a-chieved from any of the parking lots. We suggest beginning at lot P1. Hike northward on the **Shoreline Trail (ST)** to lot P3 and then continue northeastward on the **Boundary Trail (BT)**. This trail can be followed across the north end of the Conservation Area and down the east shore of Little Dixie Lake to lot P2 (see map). From here, pick up the **Shoreline Trail**, cross the dam and return to your car.

A crisp autumn day at Little Dixie Lake

A view from the Shoreline Trail

18 BEAR CREEK TRAIL

DISTANCE: DAYHIKES OF 1-5 MILES
TERRAIN: FLAT TO HILLY
DIFFICULTY: EASY TO MODERATE
WALKING TIME: 1/2-4 HRS.

Bear Creek, a tributary of Perche Creek, flows westward across the northern edge of Columbia. The City is establishing a green-belt along much of its course and dayhikers can chose from a variety of routes that lead through the Creek's valley. **Trailheads** are located on Garth Ave., on Creasy Springs Road and at the Cosmo Recreation Area. A separate fitness trail circles a tributary of Bear Creek at **Albert-Oakland Park**. Additional trail sections and access points should become available in the future as the Bear Creek Greenbelt expands.

Directions: To reach the **Garth Ave. trailhead**, take the Providence Road Exit from I-70 (Exit 126). Turn south, proceed to Business Loop 70 and turn right (west). Drive 1 block and turn right (north) on Garth Ave. The trailhead will be 1 mile ahead, on your left.

To reach the **Creasy Springs Road trailhead**, take Exit 125 from I-70, proceed to the north side of the highway and turn right on Creasy Springs Road. The trailhead will be 1.3 miles ahead, on your left.

To reach the **Cosmo Recreation Area trailhead**, take Exit 125 from I-70 and proceed west on Business Loop 70 for almost 1 mile to the Park entrance, on your right. Drive straight back to the north end of the Park where the Bear Creek Trailhead will be found near the Skate Park.

To reach the **Albert-Oakland Park fitness trail**, take the Range Line St. Exit (Exit 127) from I-70 and drive north on U.S. 763. Proceed to Blue Ridge Road and turn right. Drive another mile to Oakland Gravel Road and turn right (south). The Park entrance will be a short distance, on your right.

Routes: The map on page 65 provides an overview of the Bear Creek Trail network and its various trailheads. We suggest a number of dayhikes utilizing this network, ranging from 1 to 5 miles in length.

Albert Oakland Fitness Trail. This 1 mile loop is a paved walkway which follows a tributary of Bear Creek, running along and through a frisbee-golf course. Exercise stations are spaced along the route and the

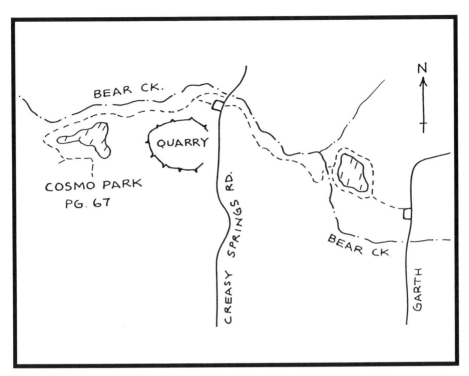

BEAR CREEK TRAIL NETWORK

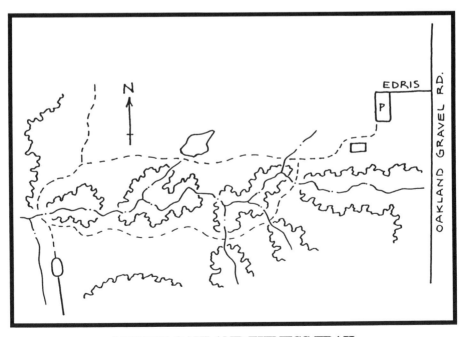

ALBERT-OAKLAND FITNESS TRAIL

65

trail crosses a pleasing mix of natural habitat. A pond, open meadows and a streamside woodland characterize the area.

Bear Creek Trail (Garth Ave. to Cosmo Park). From the Garth Ave. trailhead (see directions), the Bear Creek Trail leads westward and soon splits to circle a large wetland. Birdwatchers may find rails, bitterns, herons and a variety of songbirds in this marsh. Just west of this scenic wetland the main trail curves to the south, crosses Bear Creek and then follows the stream to the northwest.

Angling away from the creek, the path crosses Creasy Springs Road, cuts through the new access lot and then continues westward above the south bank of Bear Creek. The route skirts the north edge of a quarry and soon enters a broad valley where a series of ponds and marshes border the stream. As the valley begins to narrow, the path curves back to the southeast and intersects the trail network of Cosmo Park (see map on page 67). The roundtrip hike from Garth Ave. to this junction is approximately 3 miles.

Bear Creek Trail at Cosmo Park. A network of **hiking trails (HT)** provides a variety of potential dayhikes within Cosmo Park. Furthermore, the **Rhett Walters Memorial Bike Trail (BT)**, designed for mountain bikes, intersects the hiking trail network, yielding additional routes for cautious hikers. We suggest a 2-mile loop, described below and illustrated on the map, which uses the hiking trails and passes some of the more interesting natural features.

From the trailhead, hike northward and descend into the forest. Continue straight ahead at the first intersection, soon hiking above the south shore of a **woodland lake**. Turn north along its east shore, cross a roadway and begin a winding descent to a forest stream, crossing the bike trail at two points along the way. Once past the stream, the path climbs to the edge of an **old quarry (Q)**. After inspecting the quarry, hike above its eastern edge and watch for a cutoff to the right; this trail leads down to a **boardwalk** which leads across a scenic wetland of the Bear Creek Valley.

Exiting the wetland, the trail enters a clearing at the end of the Park's service road. Across this clearing, both the Bike Trail and the Hiking Trail continue westward; the latter soon forks with the main path curving down to Bear Creek and then leading upstream to the Creasy Springs Road and Garth Ave. trailheads (see overview map and discussion above). Bear left at the fork, cross the Bike Trail and begin a winding ascent back to the Service Road (see map on next page). Turn right on the service road and then return to the trailhead via a path that leads southward along the edge of the golf course.

66

The wetland boardwalk at Cosmo Park

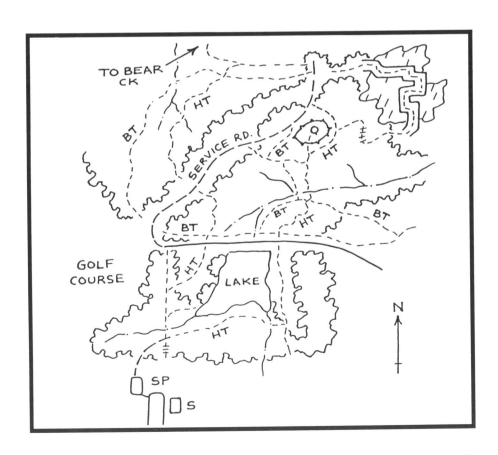

TO BEAR CK

BT

HT

SERVICE RD.

BT

HT

BT

BT

HT

BT

GOLF COURSE

HT

LAKE

HT

N

SP

S

19 GRINDSTONE NATURE AREA

NORTH LOOP
   DISTANCE: 2.5 MILES
   TERRAIN: HILLY
   DIFFICULTY: MODERATE
   WALKING TIME: 2 HRS.

SOUTH LOOP
   DISTANCE: 2 MILES
   TERRAIN: HILLY
   DIFFICULTY: MODERATE
   WALKING TIME: 1.5 HRS.

The junction of Grindstone Creek and Hinkson Creek, in southeast Columbia, is a landscape of rock bluffs, hillside forest and valley meadows. Protected within the **Grindstone Nature Area**, this is an excellent destination for hikers. A gravel roadway now leads through the center of the preserve, connecting the Old 63 and Capen Park trailheads, and a network of foot trails provides access to more secluded retreats within the 230 acre refuge.

Directions: From U.S. 63 on the east side of Columbia, take the Stadium Blvd. Exit and head west. Proceed to Old 63 (the first major intersection) and turn left (south). The Nature Area entrance will be approximately .5 mile ahead, on your right.

Routes: There are numerous potential dayhikes within the Grindstone Nature Area. We suggest the following loops.
   North Loop (N). This 2.5 mile loop begins and ends at the Old 63 trailhead, on the east side of the preserve. From the parking lot, hike southward and then westward on the gravel road, crossing Grindstone Creek. Turn right at the old water tank and ascend to the **limestone bluffs** above Grindstone Creek (see map); this rock is part of the Burlington Formation, dating from the Mississippian Period. Hike northward atop the cliffs and then descend westward through the forest. Angle to the northwest at the next junction, bypassing short cutoffs on your left; pick up a trail which climbs to the bluffs above Hinkson Creek (see map) and walk northward above the cliffs before descending to the creek valley on the longer, northernmost path.
   Nearing the Capen Park bridge, turn left on a trail that crosses through the Grindstone **prairie**. Controlled burns are used to re-establish and maintain this native grassland which explodes with wildflowers in late summer. Watch for meadowlarks, dickcissels, eastern bluebirds and eastern kingbirds in this area. Red-tailed hawks and turkey vultures often soar above the grassland which is home to a variety of small mammals. Continue southeastward to the gravel road and return to the parking lot.

Bluffs along Grindstone Creek

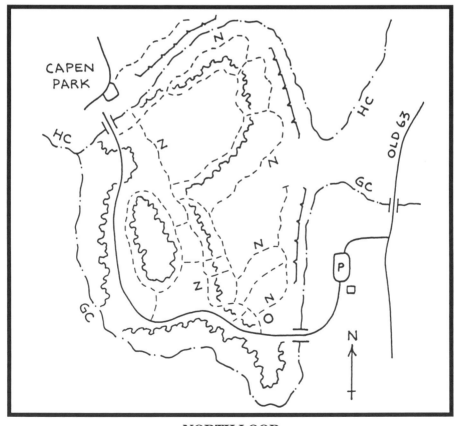

NORTH LOOP

South Loop (S). This 2 mile loop also begins and ends at the Old 63 trail-head, on the east side of the preserve. From the parking lot, hike south-ward on the gravel road, cross Grindstone Creek and turn left (south) opposite the old water tank (see map). Cross the creek once again via stepping stones and continue southward for a short distance; watch for two parallel cutoffs on your right which border the remnants of an old building. Take the second right, pass the old foundation and ascend into the forest. Bypass the next two trails, on your right, staying atop the ridge before taking the third cutoff (see map); this trail descends to the northeast, eventually arriving on the south bank of Grindstone Creek.

Turn right, hiking upstream and then curving southward along a tributary of Grindstone Creek. After crossing a branch of this creek, the trail reaches a junction. Turn left, ford another branch and then turn left at the first intersection. This path heads back toward Grindstone Creek, passing an old burr oak (x) along the way. Cross the creek and continue straight ahead, soon intersecting the gravel road. Turn right and return to the parking lot.

A view from the South Loop

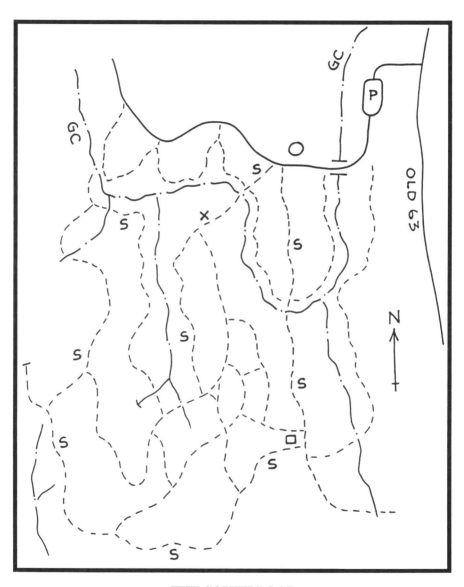

THE SOUTH LOOP

20 MKT TRAIL

DISTANCE: DAYHIKES OF 2-9 MILES
TERRAIN: FLAT
DIFFICULTY: EASY
WALKING TIME: 1-6 HRS.

Part of one of the finest rail-to-trail conversions in the United States, the **MKT Trail** extends for 8.9 miles, from downtown Columbia to its junction with the Katy Trail near McBaine, Missouri. Using the old bed of a Missouri, Kansas & Texas spur track, this wide, graded path offers an avenue for exercise and nature study in western Boone County.

Mileage markers are spaced every .5 mile along the trail and access lots are provided throughout the city of Columbia. A series of fine bridges carry the trail across Flat Branch, Hinkson and Perche Creeks as it gradually descends to the Missouri River floodplain. The route passes through a superb variety of natural habitat including upland forest, open meadows and valley wetlands; as a result, observant hikers are sure to see an excellent diversity of wildlife along the trail.

Directions: The best access points for non-locals are at the Martin Luther King Jr. Memorial Garden, on Stadium Blvd., at the Forum Nature Area, on Forum Blvd., and at the Scott Blvd. Access Lot. The western end of the Trail can be accessed from the Katy Trail lot, in McBaine. The overview map on page 73 illustrates their locations.

To reach the **Martin Luther King Jr. Memorial Garden**, take Exit 124 (Stadium Blvd.) from I-70. Head south on Stadium Blvd. and drive 3 miles to the Garden entrance, on your right. The Trail mileage from downtown Columbia is 1.4 miles at this lot.

To reach the **Forum Nature Area** access lot, take Exit 124 from I-70. Drive south on Stadium Blvd. and proceed 2.5 miles. Turn right on Forum Blvd. and drive another 1.1 miles to the Nature Area, on your right. The Trail mileage from downtown Columbia is 2.7 miles at this lot.

To reach the **Scott Blvd. access lot**, take Exit 124 from I-70. Drive south on Stadium Blvd. and proceed 1 mile. Turn right on Broadway and continue on this road as it curves southward and becomes Scott Blvd. The access lot will be 4.2 miles from Stadium Blvd. The Trail mileage from downtown Columbia is 4.7 miles at this lot.

To reach the **McBaine lot** for the Katy Trail, take Exit 126 from I-70 and drive south on Providence Road. Proceed 5.5 miles to the south edge of the city and bear right onto Route K. Drive another 7.5 miles to McBaine. The MKT/Katy Trail junction is approximately .3 mile north of the McBaine lot.

One of many fine bridges on the MKT Trail

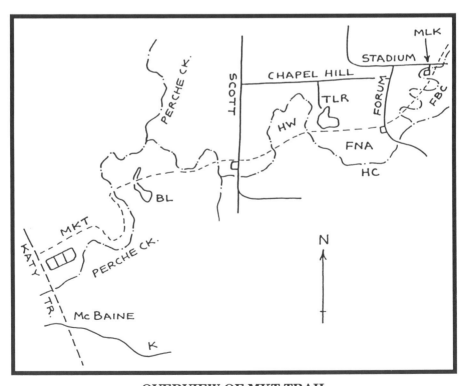

OVERVIEW OF MKT TRAIL

Routes: Since mileage markers are spaced along the MKT trail, one can design any hike that may be dictated by time constraints or their level of fitness. We suggest the following dayhikes.

MLK Garden to Forum Nature Area. The section of the MKT trail between the MLK Garden, on Stadium Blvd., and the Forum Nature Area covers 1.3 miles (2.6 miles roundtrip); if one includes a walk through the Nature Area itself, the roundtrip hike will total 4.6 miles. Most of the MKT in this section follows the corridor of Flat Branch Creek, crossing the stream several times via a series of fine, wooden bridges. The trail passes through a rich, upland forest for the first half of its route, followed by an area of wooded meadows and golf course vistas.

Crossing under Forum Blvd. the MKT reaches the **Forum Nature Area** lot. Those wanting to tour the Nature Area should cut through the lot and pick up the path that leads southward and then westward. A double-loop, covering 2 miles, takes you past riparian woodlands, across the central grasslands and around seasonal wetlands. Bluebird boxes dot the meadows and dickcissels are common here during the warmer months. If rainfall has been adequate, the shallow wetlands attract a variety of herons, bitterns and waterfowl. Kingfishers, indigo buntings, northern bobwhites, American kestrels, red-tailed hawks and American goldfinches are among the resident birds. Late-day visitors may spot whitetailed deer or red fox on the meadows.

Forum Nature Area to Scott Blvd. This 2 mile hike (4 miles roundtrip) follows the MKT trail through the Hinkson Creek Valley. Along the way it passes the **Forum Nature Area** (see description above), **Twin Lakes Recreation Area** and the **Hinkson Woods Conservation Area**. The latter is tucked into a bend of Hinkson Creek; its woodlands and meadows are accessed by a network of foot trails, some of which are overgrown during the summer months. Beyond the Conservation Area, the MKT parallels the creek at a distance and eventually reaches the Scott Blvd. lot.

Scott Blvd. lot to McBaine. This 4.5 mile section of the MKT (including a .3 mile portion of the Katy Trail) yields a roundtrip hike of 9 miles. From Scott Blvd., the MKT heads west, crossing Hinkson Creek and then skirting two of its meanders. It then crosses a large, open grassland before reaching Brushwood Lake, a shallow, secluded wetland. Just beyond this lake the trail crosses Perche Creek via an old railroad bridge and then turn south, paralleling the stream and its woodlands. This section of the trail was diverted southward, clearing the way for expansion of Columbia's wastewater wetlands. These wetlands provide natural filters which clean the water before it is returned to the Missouri River. Once past these marshlands the MKT intersects the Katy Trail. Turn left (south) for a .3 mile walk to the McBaine lot (see overview map on page 73).

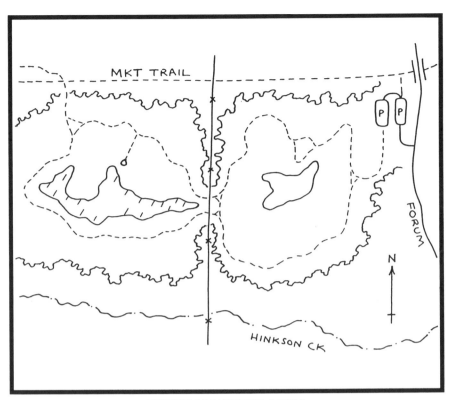

FORUM NATURE AREA

A winter day at Forum Nature Area

75

21 ROCK BRIDGE MEMORIAL STATE PARK

DISTANCE: DAYHIKES OF 1.75-5.0 MILES
TERRAIN: ROLLING TO HILLY
DIFFICULTY: EASY TO MODERATE
WALKING TIME: 1-3.5 HRS.

Combine a thick layer of soluble bedrock and the relatively abundant precipitation of the American Midwest and you get the varied "karst" topography of **Rock Bridge Memorial State Park**, just south of Columbia. This 2238 acre preserve boasts a fascinating collection of caves, bluffs, sinkholes, springs and a rock bridge, all carved from Burlington Limestone (Mississippian age) by Gans Creek and its many tributaries. Add to these features a rich hardwood forest and restored grasslands and you get a scenic wonderland for naturalists and weekend explorers. Furthermore, the entire refuge is accessed by an excellent network of trails, making Rock Bridge Memorial State Park a superb destination for hikers. More trails run through the Gans Creek Wild Area, described in Chapter 22, which is just east of the Park.

The most famous and popular features of Rock Bridge Memorial State Park are the **Rock Bridge (RB)** itself and the **Devil's Icebox Cave (DIB)**. The bridge is a remnant of a collapsed cave roof while the latter, a cool retreat for both humans and gray bats, is the mouth of an underground stream.

Directions: From I-70 in Columbia, take the Providence Road Exit (Exit 126); this is Missouri Route 163. Drive south for 5.5 miles and turn left on Route 163 as it branches from Route K. Follow Route 163 to parking areas as illustrated on the overview map.

Alternatively, from U.S. 63 southeast of Columbia, turn west on Route 163 and drive 3 miles to the Karst Trailhead or 3.5 miles to Pierpont (see map).

Routes: The fine network of trails at Rock Bridge Memorial State Park offers a large number of potential dayhikes. We suggest the routes described below.

Karst Trail (KT). This 1.75 mile loop begins and ends at the Karst Trailhead on Fox Lane, .5 mile east of Pierpont and just south of Route 163. The route crosses a "karst plain" devoid of surface streams but studded with numerous sinkholes. These collapsed caves drain water into underground streams and, during periods of wet weather, may become ponds themselves. Much of the plain is covered by grassland while islands of trees cluster around the sinkholes.

Red arrows mark the main trail loop; those not wishing to complete the entire route can use a **connector trail (CT)**, blazed with white arrows, which shorten the hike.

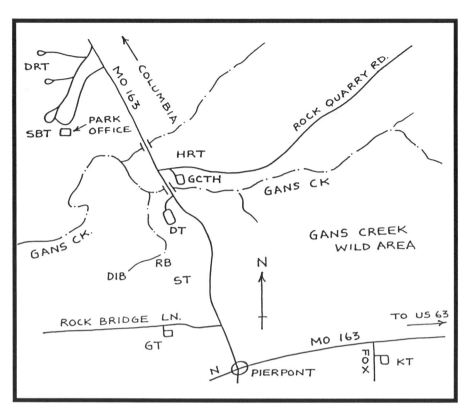

OVERVIEW OF ROCK BRIDGE MEMORIAL STATE PARK

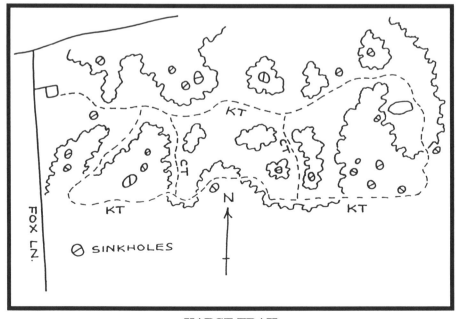

KARST TRAIL

Combined Loop: Deer Run (DRT) and **Spring Brook (SBT) Trails**. This combined loop hike begins and ends at the Deer Run Trailhead, in the northwest section of the Park, and yields a dayhike of 5 miles. Follow the northernmost arm of the **Deer Run Trail** (blazed with yellow arrows) as it leads westward and then southward along the Park's boundary, hugging the fenceline of a cattle ranch. Dropping to the floodplain of Gans Creek, the trail forks; bear right, passing beneath limestone bluffs and then hiking southward to the north bank of the creek.

The Deer Run Trail now turns eastward along Gans Creek; bypass the first connector, staying along the creek, and watch for the junction with the **Spring Brook Trail**, blazed with red arrows. If stream conditions permit, cross Gans Creek and follow the Spring Brook Trail as it climbs along a tributary and then levels out atop the ridge. Turn left at the trail junction, hiking toward the Devil's Icebox. Bypass the white Connector Trail (CT), continuing to the **Icebox/Natural Bridge area**, which is served by a separate trail loop (see map).

The north arm of the **Spring Brook Trail** leaves the Devil's Icebox parking lot and descends back to the Gans Creek floodplain along a sidestream; bypass cutoffs to the Gans Creek trailhead and to the white Connector Trail. The Spring Brook Trail hugs the edge of the floodplain and then recrosses Gans Creek via a bridge. It then leads westward to the east arm of the **Deer Run Trail (DRT)**; turn right and climb along a tributary to the Deer Run Trailhead (see map).

Gans Creek

78

Rock outcrops along the Deer Run Trail

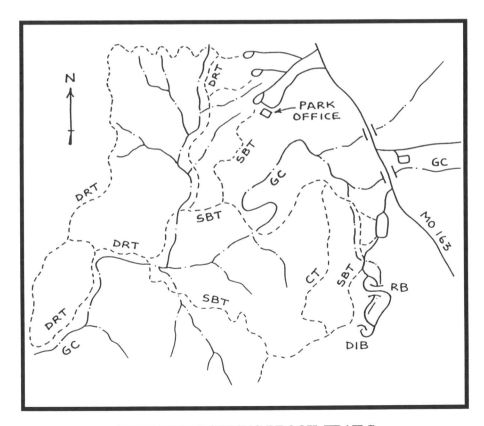

DEER RUN & SPRING BROOK TRAILS

High Ridge Trail (HRT). This 2.3 mile loop begins and ends at the Gans Creek Trailhead (GCTH), on Rock Quarry Road, .7 miles south of the Park Office entry road (see overview map). The trail climbs northward and soon forks. Bear right and begin a gradual ascent to the crest of the ridge where a white Connector Trail (CT) offers a short cut back to the trailhead. Continue along the High Ridge Trail, blazed with blue arrows, hiking northeastward atop the ridge. Views extend southward into the Gans Creek Wild Area (see Chapter 22) and westward across much of the Park. Bypass several cutoffs (see map) and follow the main trail as it curves to the northwest and descends into the Clear Creek valley. It then follows this stream toward the southwest before curving back to the trailhead.

Sinkhole and Grassland Trails. Combining these two trails yields a dayhike of 3.5 miles. From the Devil's Icebox Trailhead (DT) lot, hike southward on the **Sinkhole Trail (ST)** which is blazed with green arrows. Bear left at the fork, gradually climbing along a stream. Near the upper reaches of this creek the trail curves westward and passes a cluster of sinkholes before intersecting the white **Connector Trail (CT)**. Turn left here and hike southward to the Grassland Trailhead (GTH) on Rock Bridge Lane (see map).

Hike the **Grassland Trail (GT)** loop in either direction, passing a large number of ponds and sinkholes. Native grasses have been restored in this area where the thin, rocky soil keeps the forest at bay. Less tolerant of these dry conditions, trees cluster near the sinkholes and along the lone stream bed. As you hike the loop, look and listen for grassland species such as meadowlarks, eastern bluebirds, northern bobwhites and field sparrows. Red-tailed hawks, American kestrels and great-horned owls patrol the area and turkey vultures often soar above the prairie. Resident mammals include red fox, coyotes, white-tailed deer, ground squirrels, skunk, cottontail rabbits, prairie voles and pocket gophers.

Complete the Grassland Trail loop and follow the Connector Trail back to the **Sinkhole Trail (ST)**. Turn left (west) on this path, snaking past more ponds and sinkholes and gradually curving back to the northeast. Turn left (north) at the junction with the white Connector Trail and begin a long, gradual descent back to the Devil's Icebox Trailhead.

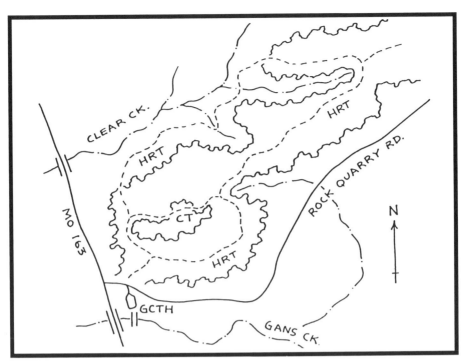

HIGH RIDGE TRAIL

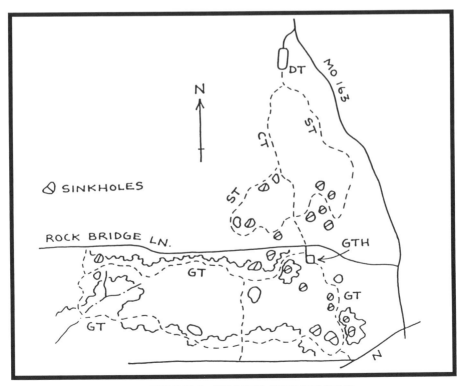

SINKHOLE & GRASSLAND TRAILS

22 GANS CREEK WILD AREA

NORTHEAST LOOP
  DISTANCE: 3 MILES
  TERRAIN: HILLY
  DIFFICULTY: MODERATE
  WALKING TIME: 2 HRS.

SOUTHEAST LOOP
  DISTANCE: 2.8 MILES
  TERRAIN: HILLY
  DIFFICULTY: MODERATE
  WALKING TIME: 2 HRS.

CENTRAL LOOP
  DISTANCE: 3.6 MILES
  TERRAIN: HILLY
  DIFFICULTY: MODERATE
  WALKING TIME: 2.5 HRS

WEST LOOP
  DISTANCE: 2 MILES
  TERRAIN: HILLY
  DIFFICULTY: MODERATE
  WALKING TIME: 1.5 HRS.

Just upstream from the natural wonders of Rock Bridge Memorial State Park is the scenic gorge of Gans Creek, surrounded by 750 acres of forest, rock bluffs, cedar glades and meadows. A fine network of trails provides access to the **Gans Creek Wild Area**, crossing the valley walls, running along the stream and leading out to spectacular overlooks.

Directions: There are three primary trailheads for the Gans Creek Wild Area. The **Gans Creek Trailhead (GCTH)** is on Rock Quarry Road, just east of Missouri 163, 1.5 miles southeast of Columbia (1.2 miles north of Pierpont).

To reach the **Wagon Wheel Trailhead (WWT)**, take the Route AC exit from U.S. 63, east of Columbia. Drive west on AC (Nifong Road) for 1.2 miles to Rock Quarry Road. Turn left (south) on Rock Quarry and drive 1 mile to Gans Road. Turn left (east) on Gans Road, proceed .5 mile and turn right (south) on Bearfield Road. The trailhead lot will be .5 mile ahead.

To reach the **Shooting Star Trailhead (SST)**, take the Route 163 exit from U.S. 63, southeast of Columbia. Drive west on 163 for 2.6 miles and turn right (north) on Bonne Femme Church Road. The trailhead will be .3 miles ahead, on your left.

Routes: There are numerous potential dayhike routes at Gans Creek Wild Area. We suggest the following loop hikes; the terminology used is purely descriptive.

Northeast Loop (NE). This 3 mile loop begins and ends at the Wagon Wheel Trailhead (WWT). Take the trail which angles to the SSE (see map) and descend gradually toward Gans Creek. Turn left at the fork, hiking through a cedar glade and then curving northward and climbing above limestone cliffs. The trail continues to the northeast, crosses a tributary of Gans Creek and then descends southwestward to cross the primary channel.

Once across Gans Creek, the trail climbs steadily to the southeast, lev-

The Coyote Bluff Overlook

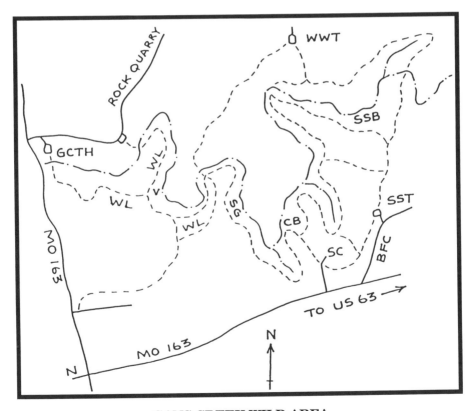

GANS CREEK WILD AREA

els out and intersects another trail. Turn right, soon arriving at the **Shooting Star Bluff (SSB)** where several overlooks yield views into and across the gorge. Continue westward from the bluffs, gradually descending to Gans Creek. Cross the stream, bear left at the next intersection and climb back to the Wagon Wheel Trailhead.

Southeast Loop (SE). This 2.8 mile loop begins and ends at the Shooting Star Trailhead (SST). Hike northward from the parking lot, bypassing cutoffs on your left and right. A short distance past the second cutoff you will reach the **Shooting Star Bluff (SSB)**, described above. Descend westward to Gans Creek and then bear left, curving southward and paralleling the stream for almost .5 mile. The trail then makes a long loop to the southeast in order to cross a feeder stream and climbs out of the gorge.

Levelling out atop the ridge, the trail reaches an intersection. Turn left for a short walk out to **Coyote Bluff (CB)**, an isolated overlook atop the Gans Creek Gorge. After enjoying the view, backtrack to the southeast, bypass the trail on your left and continue out to the **Special Use Camp (SC)**. Cross through the clearing and pick up the trail which leads back to the Shooting Star Trailhead (see map), bypassing a cutoff on your left along the way.

Central Loop (CL). This 3.6 mile loop begins and ends at the Wagon Wheel Trailhead (WWT). Hike to the southwest for a long, gradual descent to Gans Creek. Cross the stream and turn left, hiking upstream and soon climbing above the limestone cliffs. This rocky ridge and open woodland is known as **Saunder's Glade (SG)**; we feel it is one of the more scenic sites in the Wild Area. Continue southeastward atop the ridge until the trail loops around a sidestream and cuts back to **Coyote Bluff (CB)**, a spectacular overlook atop limestone cliffs.

From the Bluff, hike southeastward and turn left at the first intersection, gradually descending through another sidestream valley and returning to the floor of the gorge. Hike upstream along Gans Creek for almost .5 mile and, at the trail intersection, cross the stream. Bear left at the next junction and climb back to the Wagon Wheel Trailhead.

West Loop (WL). This 2 mile loop begins and ends at the Gans Creek Trailhead (GCTH). Hike eastward on Rock Quarry Road for .2 mile and pick up a trail that enters the Wild Area at a small pulloff (see map on page 83). The trail crosses Gans Creek and then heads upstream along the floor of the gorge. After following the stream for .5 mile the trail cuts away from Gans Creek and climbs steeply onto the limestone rim. Here it reaches an **overlook (V)** and a trail intersection.

Turn left, hiking above the cliffs and bear left at the next junction, descending back to the valley floor. Turn right at this intersection, hiking southward from Gans Creek and climbing along one of its tributaries. This trail segment curves back to join the ridgetop trail; turn right and and then bear left at the next junction, hiking westward atop the gorge before making a long, gradual descent to the Gans Creek Trailhead.

84

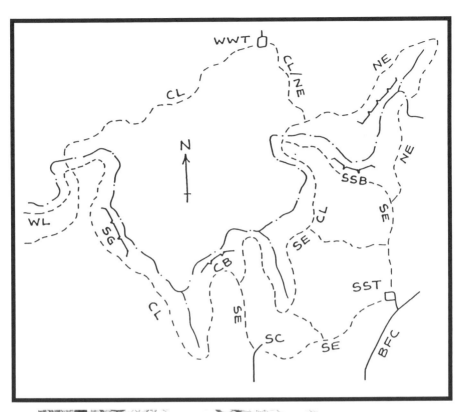

Along Gans Creek

23 EAGLE BLUFFS CONSERVATION AREA

NORTHEAST LOOP
  DISTANCE: 2.5 MILES
  TERRAIN: FLAT
  DIFFICULTY: EASY
  WALKING TIME: 1.5 HRS.

WEST LOOP
  DISTANCE: 4 MILES
  TERRAIN: FLAT
  DIFFICULTY: EASY
  WALKING TIME: 2.5 HRS.

SOUTH LOOP
  DISTANCE: 5 MILES
  TERRAIN: FLAT
  DIFFICULTY: EASY
  WALKING TIME: 3 HRS.

One can hardly imagine an area more attractive to migrant waterbirds (and to the birders who watch them) than **Eagle Bluffs Conservation Area**, southwest of Columbia. This 4269 acre refuge, which stretches for five miles along the Missouri River floodplain, is a mosaic of channels, marshlands, ponds, meadows and bottomland timber. Access is provided by a network of gravel roads, levees and field trails; in addition, a five-mile segment of the Katy Trail (see Chapter 26) runs along the east edge of the preserve.

Bald eagles winter here and large flocks of migrant waterfowl visit the refuge during spring and fall migrations. Other migrants include white-faced ibis, American white pelicans, ospreys and a wide variety of shorebirds. Summer brings a mix of herons, egrets, rails and bitterns to Eagle Bluffs and flooded timber provides nest sites for great blue herons, red-headed woodpeckers, belted kingfishers and wood ducks. Trumpeter swams were recently released here in an effort to restore migrant populations to the Missouri River valley.

Visitors should note that much of the refuge is closed from October 15 through the end of waterfowl season.

Directions: From I-70 in Columbia, take the Providence Road Exit (Exit 126) and drive south through the city. Proceed 5.5 miles and continue southwestward on Route K. Drive 7.5 miles to McBaine; the Eagle Bluffs Conservation Area stretches southward from Route K and is accessed via Star School Road (see map).

86

Floodplain woodlands border much of the refuge

Shallow wetlands attract waterfowl and shorebirds

Routes: The graveled roads, levees and field trails of this Conservation Area permit a large variety of potential dayhikes. We suggest the following loops; terminology is purely descriptive.

Northeast Loop (NE). This 2.5 mile loop begins and ends at parking lot P1 (see map). Hike northeastward from the lot atop a levee, crossing open meadows and seasonal wetlands. Turn right (south) at the trail junctions, hiking along Perche Creek and its associated woodlands. Several ponds dot the timber; watch for red-headed woodpeckers, kingfishers and great blue herons in this area. Turn right at the next trail intersection and continue westward to the gravel road, bypassing several levees along the way. Turkey vultures and red-tailed hawks often roost in the trees that line this route. Turn right and hike along the roadway, checking the channel on your left for herons, shorebirds and waterfowl. Turn right once again at the road intersection and return to your car (see map).

West Loop (WL). This 4 mile loop begins and ends at lot P2 (see map). Hike southward on the levee that borders the woodland, continuing straight ahead at the first trail junction. Further along, an old river channel winds through the timber and parallels the levee. This is an excellent area to look for great blue herons, green-backed herons, black-crowned night herons, red-headed woodpeckers and belted kingfishers. A variety of water-loving songbirds will also be found.

Turn left (east) on the levee that parallels the gravel road, passing a series of ponds, sloughs and seasonal wetlands. The levee turns northward, angling away from the road and crossing a mosaic of meadow, marsh and shrubland. Bypass cutoffs on your left and right, eventually heading northwest and returning to lot P2. A bird blind (B) sits along the levee near the end of your loop hike.

South Loop (SL). This 5 mile loop begins and ends at lot P3 (see map). Hike eastward along a treeline, curving to the southeast and passing a wooded lake. Continue straight ahead through the intersection and curve eastward to join the Perche Creek levee. Hike southeastward atop this levee, proceeding to the tip of the refuge; ponds and sloughs in this area often attract a good variety of shorebirds.

The levee turns southwestward and then parallels the Missouri River toward the WNW. Bypass cutoffs on your right, hiking along the bottomland timber that borders the river. Migrant songbirds often congregate in these woods during spring and early autumn. Continue northwestward to the gravel road, turn right and follow the roadway back to your car.

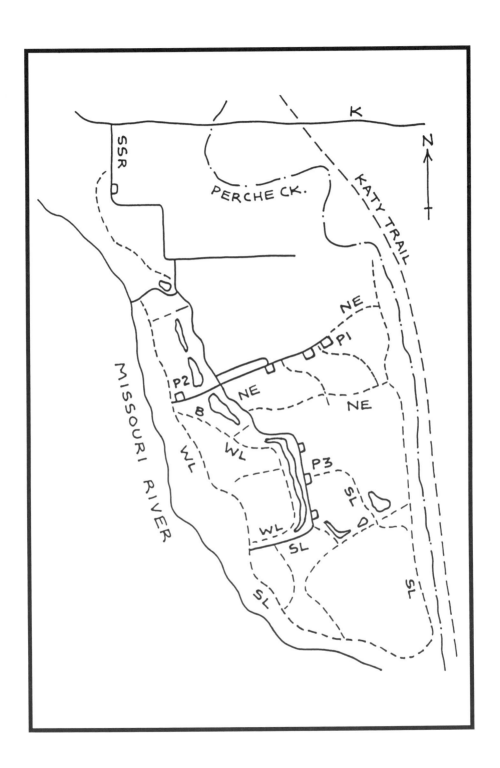

24 THREE CREEKS CONSERVATION AREA

RIDGE TRAIL
  DISTANCE: 2.5-3.5 MILES RT
  TERRAIN: ROLLING, A HILL
  DIFFICULTY: EASY-MODERATE
  WALKING TIME: 2-2.5 HRS.

TURKEY CREEK NATURE TRAIL
  DISTANCE: 1.7-2.7 MILES
  TERRAIN: HILLY
  DIFFICULTY: MODERATE
  WALKING TIME: 1.5-2 HRS.

The junction of Bonne Femme, Turkey and Bass Creeks in south-central Boone County is the site of this scenic, 1479 acre Conservation Area. Steep-walled ridges and deep valleys characterize the preserve which offers some excellent hiking opportunities. A central jeep road, referred to as the Ridge Trail in this guide, winds out to spectacular overlooks while the Nature Trail loops across the north wall of the Turkey Creek gorge and leads down to the valley floor.

Directions: From U.S. 63, approximately 4 miles south of Columbia, turn west at Deer Park; this Exit is .3 miles south of the Route 163 Exit. Follow Deer Park Road as it zigzags toward the southwest; the Three Creeks Conservation Area will be 2.2 miles ahead.

Routes: As mentioned above, there are two primary hiking routes at Three Creeks. We suggest the following dayhikes.

Ridge Trail (RT). This wide path leaves the west end of the parking lot and leads southwestward across open meadows. Bypass the cutoff to the Turkey Creek Nature Trail, on your left and a second cutoff, on your right. Eastern bluebirds are common on the ridgetop meadows and white-tailed deer browse in these clearings at dawn and dusk. A pond, across from the second cutoff, fills with peepers in early spring and attracts a variety of wildlife throughout the year.

One of several overlooks along the Ridge Trail

Turkey Creek rumbles through its gorge

As you continue southwestward the ridge begins to narrow and trailside clearings yield spectacular views into the adjacent valleys; the Turkey Creek gorge is just south of the ridge while Bonne Femme Creek has carved a deep, narrow valley to the north. Turkey vultures often soar above the overlooks (V) at midday, catching updrafts along the ridge. Nearing the end of the ridge, the trail begins to descend. Those wishing to avoid any hill climbs should return to the lot from this point, completing a roundtrip hike of 2.5 miles.

Fit and adventurous hikers may want to continue westward as the trail descends from the ridge via a rather steep jog to the north and then forks. Turn left at the fork and hike across the valley floor to the junction of Bass and Turkey Creeks. Your roundtrip hike from this creekside destination is approximately 3.5 miles.

Turkey Creek Nature Trail (NT). This 2.7 mile loop hike begins and ends at the parking area. Hike eastward from the lot on a path marked by a "foot trail" sign; this is the Nature Trail (see map). The trail gradually curves to the southeast, crossing two other paths, and then turns westward to parallel Turkey Creek. At the next junction, continue straight ahead, crossing the stream four times within the next 1/4 mile.

Just after the fourth crossing, the trail forks; a right turn takes you on the Connector Trail (CT), which shortens the hike to 1.7 miles. Those who wish to complete the entire trail should bear left (straight) at this intersection, continuing westward along Turkey Creek. As the trail curves southward, you will cross the stream two more times. The route then angles back to the north for a steady climb out of the gorge. Turn left at the junction with the Connector Trail, hike out to the Ridge Trail and turn right; the parking lot will be a short distance ahead.

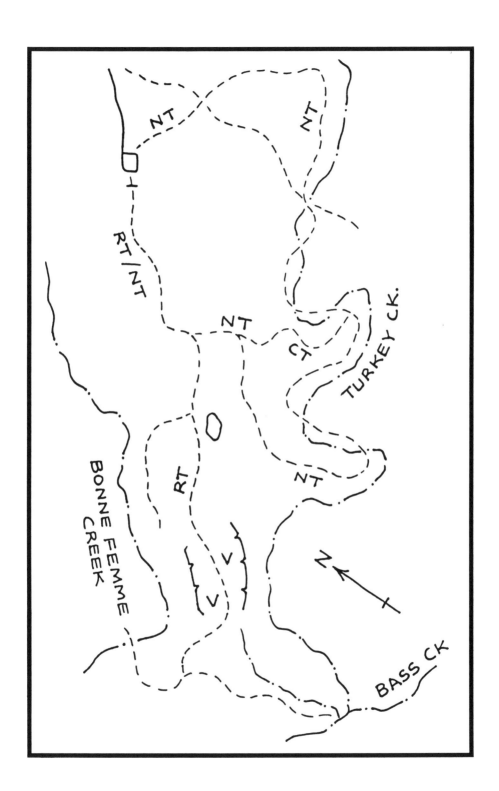

NT

NT

RT/NT

NT

CT

TURKEY CK.

NT

BONNE FEMME CREEK

RT

N

BASS CK

93

25 CEDAR CREEK RANGER DISTRICT

DISTANCE: DAYHIKES OF 2.4 -8.0 MILES
TERRAIN: ROLLING TO HILLY
DIFFICULTY: EASY TO MODERATE
WALKING TIME: 1.5 TO 5 HRS.

Purchased by the U.S. Soil Conservation Service during the early 1940s, the 15,000 acres of the Mark Twain National Forest's **Cedar Creek District** is now a popular destination for hikers, mountain bikers, horseback riders and hunters alike. Restored forest and grasslands characterize the preserve which is accessed by a large network of trails and gravel roads. The District is located east of U.S. 63, between the cities of Columbia, Ashland and Fulton.

The **Cedar Creek Trail (CCT)** is a 22 mile loop, blazed with gray diamonds, that winds through the southern 2/3 of the District; 1/3 of the trail's route uses graveled roads in the area. The 7-mile **Moon Trail (MT)** loops through the northwest corner of the refuge while the **Smith Creek Trail (SCT)** covers 5 miles in its north-central region; the Cedar Creek Trails Coalition was instrumental in constructing these latter two trails.

Directions: The routes described in this guide use the following trailheads. See the map on page 97 which illustrates their locations.

Pine Ridge Picnic Area (PR). This access point and picnic ground is on the north side of Route Y; from U.S. 63, at Ashland, drive east on Route Y for 6.6 miles to the entry drive, on your left.

Thomas Baskett Wildlife Research Area (TBWA). This area stretches south from Route Y, approximately 3.2 miles east of Ashland; the trail access lot is on the north side of Route Y.

Rutherford Bridge (RB). From U.S. 63, take the Columbia Regional Airport exit and drive east on Route H. Drive 4 miles to Englewood and continue east on Englewood Road for another 2.4 miles to the bridge.

Paris Fork Church (PFC). From Guthrie, drive north on Route J. Proceed 4.5 miles and turn left (west) on Road 356. Drive 1.25 miles; a small parking area is on the north side of 356, across from the Church.

Dry Fork Trailhead (DFT). Proceed to the Paris Fork Church, as described above and then turn south on Road 361. The Dry Fork Trailhead will be .9 mile ahead, on your left.

Boydsville Trailheads (BTH). From Guthrie, drive north on Route J. Proceed 5.5 miles and turn left (west) on Road 353. Turn left in Boydsville and continue to either trailhead lot, as shown on the map.

The Cedar Creek Valley

The Rutherford Bridge spans Cedar Creek

Routes: There are many potential dayhikes within the Cedar Creek Ranger District. We suggest the following routes.

Pine Ridge to Dry Fork Trailhead. From the Pine Ridge lot, cross the entry road and hike northward across high ground. Bypass a cutoff on your left and, within another .5 mile you will pass the **old Nevins Farmstead (NF)**, circa 1856. The trail then curves westward before descending to cross Dry Fork Creek (DFC); if the water is too high for a safe crossing, turn back here for a roundtrip hike of 2.4 miles.

If you are able to ford the stream, follow the trail as it crosses Road 361 and then climbs across a ridge; cedar glades cover the crest of this ridge. Another 1.5 miles brings you to the Dry Fork Trailhead. Return via the same route for a roundtrip hike of 5.4 miles.

Rutherford Bridge to Paris Fork Church. Cross Cedar Creek via the bridge (RB), curve northward and then bear right at the fork, cutting away from the old roadbed. The trail winds southward above the Cedar Creek Valley, passing a number of bluff-top overlooks and crossing Smith Creek (SC) along the way. The route eventually intersects an old dirt road which stretches from Boydsville to Cedar Creek; turn left (east) on this wide path and watch for a cutoff on your right (within .75 mile).

Turn right here, soon descending through a cedar glade and crossing a network of streams. The trail eventually climbs up to the Paris Fork Church trailhead (PFC). Return to the Rutherford Bridge from here for a roundtrip hike of 8 miles.

Smith Creek from Boydsville Trailhead. Start at the northernmost of the Boydsville trailheads and hike northwestward through the forest. This pleasant trail makes a gradual descent to the south bank of Smith Creek (SC). Return via the same route for a roundtrip hike of 2.4 miles.

Boydsville to Cedar Creek. Start at the southernmost of the Boydsville Trailheads and follow the old road bed to the west. Bypass cutoffs to the left and right and continue westward to the east bank of Cedar Creek. Return via the same route for a roundtrip hike of 3.5 miles.

Cedar Creek via the Thomas Baskett Wildlife Research Area. Park on the north side of Route Y at the TBWA trailhead (see map). Cross the road and hike southward through the Research Center, which is under the management of the University of Missouri. After leading southward for approximately 1 mile, the trail angles to the east and begins a long, gradual descent to the west bank of Cedar Creek. Return to your car via the same route for a roundtrip hike of 5 miles.

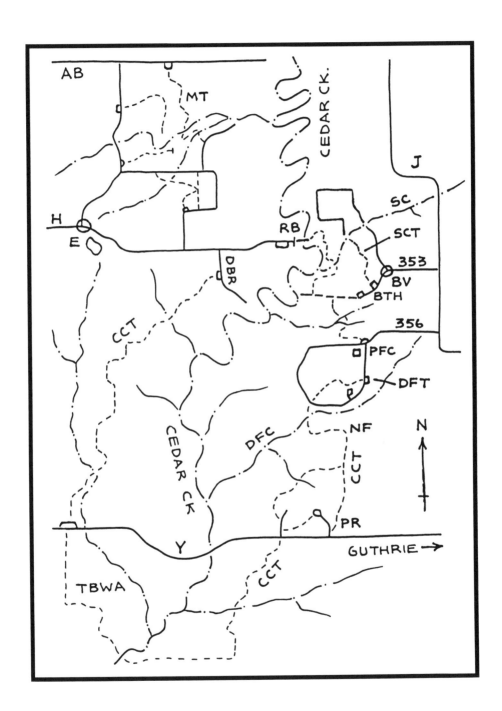

26 KATY TRAIL

DISTANCE: VARIABLE
TERRAIN: FLAT
DIFFICULTY: EASY
WALKING TIME: VARIABLE

Stretching for 200 miles from Machens (Greater St. Louis) to Sedalia, the **Katy Trail** occupies the corridor of the old Missouri-Kansas-Texas Railroad, which abandoned operations in 1986. The purchase and utilization of this scenic right-of-way was made possible by the National Trail Systems Act and aided by a generous donation from Edward D. Jones.

As mentioned above, the current route, managed as a Missouri State Park, is 200 miles in length; an additional segment, from Sedalia to Clinton, Missouri, has been donated by the Union Pacific Railroad and will bring the total distance to 233 miles. Most of the Katy Trail hugs the northern edge of the Missouri River floodplain; at Boonville, the trail leaves the river and angles southwestward across the rolling farmlands of west-central Missouri.

Any section of the Katy Trail provides a scenic and enjoyable avenue for exercise and nature study throughout the year. While we recommend specific dayhikes, described below, mileage markers are placed along the route (numbered from east to west) and one can easily tailor the distance of their hike to meet constraints of time and fitness.

Directions: There are many access points spaced along the Katy Trail. We provide directions to those trailheads that service the dayhikes recommended in this guide.

Griessen Road Trailhead (GR). From I-70, turn south on U.S. 65 toward Sedalia. Drive 15.3 miles to Route HH and turn left (east). Proceed another mile to Cedar, turn right (south) and drive 1.3 miles to Griessen Road. Turn left (east) and proceed 1.5 miles to the trailhead.

Beaman Trailhead (B). From I-70, turn south on U.S. 65 toward Sedalia. Drive 15.3 miles to Route HH and turn left (east). Proceed almost 6 miles to Beaman and turn right (south) on Route O. The small lot will be .3 mile ahead, on your right.

Rocheport Trailhead (RP). From I-70, take Exit 115. Proceed north and west on Route BB, into town.

Huntsdale Trailhead (H). From I-70, take Exit 117 and proceed south on Route O. Follow this route for approximately 6 miles to Huntsdale.

McBaine Trailhead (MB). From I-70, take Exit 126. Drive south on Providence Road (Route 163). Proceed 5.5 miles and angle southwest on Route K. Drive another 7.5 miles to McBaine.

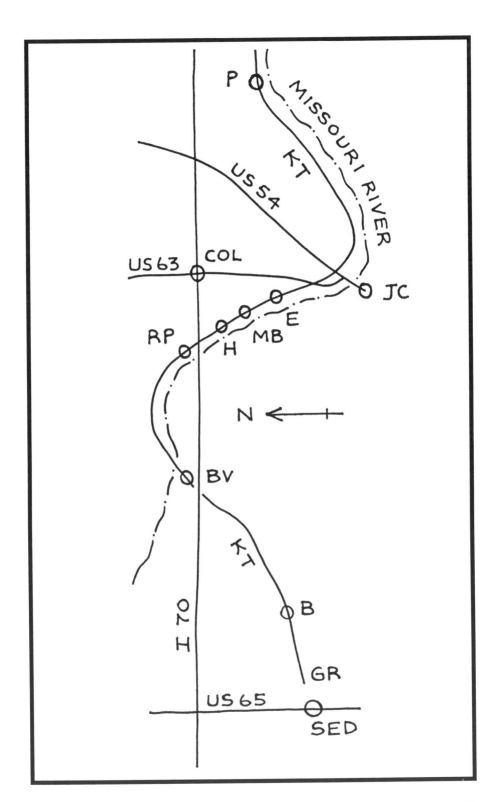

Easley Trailhead (E). From U.S. 63, just southeast of Columbia, turn west on Route 163. Proceed 3.5 miles to Pierpont and then continue westward on Route N. Follow this route all the way to Easley.

Portland Trailhead (P). From U.S. 63/U.S. 54 north of the Missouri River at Jefferson City, turn east on Route 94. Proceed 28 miles to the town of Portland. Alternatively, take Exit 161 from I-70 and drive south on Route D; Portland will be 18 miles ahead.

Routes: As discussed above, numerous access points, combined with the mileage markers along the Katy Trail, permit hikers to map out a wide variety of dayhikes. Those described below were chosen to provide an overview of the Katy Trail in Central Missouri and to take visitors to some of the Trail's more scenic segments.

Griessen Road to Beaman. This 3 mile segment of the Katy Trail runs through the Shaver Creek valley. Meadows, farmlands and riparian woodlands characterize the route. The roundtrip hike from either end is, obviously, 6 miles.

Rocheport to Huntsdale. Park at the Rocheport Trailhead and hike southeastward along the Missouri River. River views, limestone bluffs and floodplain wetlands make this segment especially scenic. Huntsdale will be 6 miles ahead (a roundtrip hike of 12 miles).

McBaine to Easley. Hike southward from McBaine. The first 5 miles of this Katy Trail segment run along the east edge of the Eagle Bluffs Conservation Area (see Chapter 23) and parallel Perche Creek. Floodplain wetlands and bottomland timber flank the trail, making this an excellent hike for birdwatchers. The roundtrip hike to Easley is 14 miles; those desiring a shorter hike can turn around at the Providence access lot (4 miles from McBaine; a roundtrip hike of 8 miles).

Portland to Bluffton. From the Portland trailhead lot, hike eastward through floodplain woodlands, across open meadows and along shallow channels of the Missouri River. This is another excellent area for wildlife observation; plan your excursion early or late in the day. The town of Bluffton is 5 miles ahead (a roundtrip hike of 10 miles).

100

The Katy Trail in the Shaver Creek Valley

Limestone bluffs rise above the Trail near Rocheport

27 BOTHWELL STATE HISTORIC SITE

DISTANCE: 1 MILE
TERRAIN: HILLY
DIFFICULTY: MODERATE
WALKING TIME: .75 HR.

Born in Maysville, Illinois, in 1848, **John Bothwell** arrived in Sedalia in 1871. There he enjoyed a varied career, serving as a lawyer, judge, banker and State Respresentative. Enamored with the scenic hills north of town, Mr. Bothwell purchased "Stoney-Ridge Farm" in 1890 and started the construction of his ridgetop home in 1897. Additions to this lodge continued into the 1920s though Bothwell himself departed for St. Louis in 1902.

Honoring John Bothwell's service to his community and to the State of Missouri, Stoney-Ridge Farm was designated a **State Historic Site** in 1974.

Directions: From I-70, take Exit 78 and drive south on U.S. 65 toward Sedalia. Drive 12.3 miles and turn left (east) on the entry road to the Bothwell State Historic Site. Proceed to the large parking area, near the Lodge.

Route: A 1-mile trail loop takes your across a wooded hillside and past several historic structures of Stoney-Ridge Farm. The trail starts near the southwest end of the parking lot (see map).

Hike southeastward into the woods and bear left at the fork. Stay on this wide path (Bothwell's old driveway) as it curves to the south and begins a steady descent into the valley. You will soon reach a fine, old gazebo (G) which offers a shady reststop along the trail.

Continue down the old driveway and, nearing the bottom of the hill, watch for a cutoff on your right. Turn onto this trail which crosses a creek, curves westward and then climbs to the north via a broad switch-back. You will reach a trail junction at the old "Gypsy Camp (GC)," another forest retreat for Bothwell's visitors. Turn left for a short climb to the Lodge area.

The Gypsy Camp

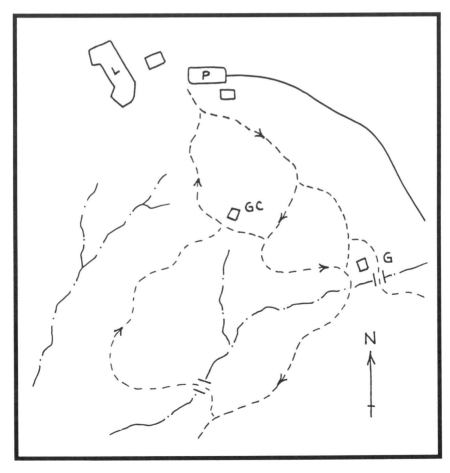

28 PRAIRIE HOME CONSERVATION AREA

DISTANCE: 5 MILE LOOP
TERRAIN: HILLY
DIFFICULTY: MODERATE
WALKING TIME: 3.5 HRS.

Molded by Schaaf Creek and its tributaries, the rolling terrain of **Prairie Home Conservation Area** is a mosaic of meadow, cropland, forest and streamside woodlands. An 8 mile Scout Trail winds through this 1461 acre preserve but some of its route is currently overgrown. We thus suggest a 5 mile loop hike, described below, which uses portions of horse trails, field access paths and the area's graveled roads.

Directions: From I-70, take Exit 107 and head south on Route 87. Drive 10 miles to Prairie Home and turn right (west) on Route J. Proceed another mile and turn left (south) on Route W. Drive 2.5 miles and turn left on a gravel road (across route W from Hunt Mill Road); proceed .4 mile to lot P2.

An alternative route from Prairie Home is to continue to the south side of town on Route 87 and then angle south on Route D. Drive 3.2 miles on Route D and turn right (west) on Cedron Road. Proceed 1 mile, bear left at the Zev Lane intersection (at the church) and then take either Cedron or Acre Road to your preferred parking area (see map).

Route: The 5 mile loop described below can be accessed from any of the parking lots (P1-P8) illustrated on the map. We begin our narrative at lot P2.

Hike southward from lot P2, climbing above the lake basin and hugging the edge of a large field. Crossing a low ridge, the trail begins a long, gradual descent to lot P8, fording small creeks along the way. Turn left on Acre Road and hike .7 mile to lot P7. Pick up the horse trail which leads northward across the edge of a meadow, paralleling Schaaf Creek. Bypass several cutoffs, staying on the main route which eventually climbs to Cedron Road. Turn right on the roadway and descend to lot P5 (see map).

Hike northward from the lot, cross Schaaf Creek and then bear left at the trail junction, fording the stream once again. Curving westward, the trail climbs from the valley and then levels out atop the ridge. Bypass the access trail from lot P4 (see map), continuing on the horse trail as it snakes to the north and descends back toward Schaaf Creek. It then turns upstream, gradually climbing along the stream and crossing several tributaries. Finally exiting the forest, the path crosses a meadow and arrives at lot P1. Turn south and hike along a dirt road to lot P3; continue south from the lot on a wide trail that yields broad views (V) to the SSE. Descend to the lake and return to lot P2.

Early spring at Prairie Home

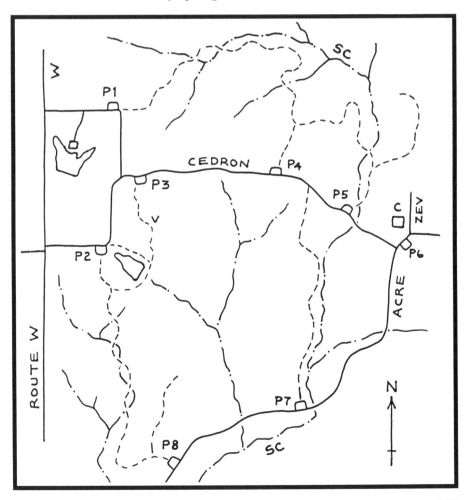

29 SCRIVNER ROAD CONSERVATION AREA

SHORT LOOP	LONG LOOP
DISTANCE: 2.75 MILES	DISTANCE: 5.75 MILES
TERRAIN: ROLLING	TERRAIN: HILLY
DIFFICULTY: EASY	DIFFICULTY: MODERATE
WALKING TIME: 2 HRS.	WALKING TIME: 3.5 HRS.

Except for the frequent gunshots that echo from its target range, **Scrivner Road Conservation Area**, in the valley of S. Moreau Creek, offers a pleasant setting for dayhikes. Ridgetop views, secluded lakes and creekside woodlands characterize this preserve, which is accessed by a fine network of bridal and hiking trails. Due to heavy horse traffic, some sections of the trail can be boggy after periods of wet weather; we thus recommend a winter visit to this Conservation Area.

Directions: From Route C, at Russellville, head south on AA. Drive 2.1 miles and turn left onto Scrivner Road. The Claywell Road turnoff will be .1 mile (on your left) while Scott Road, the primary entrance, will be 1.6 miles ahead. We suggest parking near the tractor shed (TS) at lot P1.

Routes: We suggest two loop hikes, described below.
    Short Loop (SL). This 2.75 mile loop hike begins and ends at lot P1. Hike northward on the **Ridge Trail** (our terminology), a graveled jeep road which offers broad views of the preserve; Winegar Lake lies in the valley to the west. A 1 mile hike brings you to Claywell Road where the path circles eastward, skirting lot P2. Continue straight ahead at the fork in the trail, entering the forest and soon passing a cleared picnic site.
    After exiting the forest, the trail curves to the west and reaches an intersection. Turn left, descending along the edge of a valley. Bypass cutoffs to the left and right, cross the creek and begin a gradual climb back to P1.

    Long Loop (LL). From lot P1, follow the **Ridge Trail** to lot P2, as described above. Once past the lot and farm pond, bear left at the fork. The path winds along the edge of several meadows and then descends through the forest to a trail junction. Turn left, paralleling the wood border and bypass two cutoffs on your right. Nearing a small lake, the main trail curves to the southeast and descends through a stream valley to a larger lake. Turn left at the next intersection, climbing northward to another junction; turn right (east) here and wind to the southeast, passing a scenic woodland pond. The route eventually turns south along the refuge boundary and then curves westward above S. Moreau Creek. After looping northward to cross a sidestream, the trail cuts away from the Creek, snaking across wooded meadows.

December snow blankets the refuge

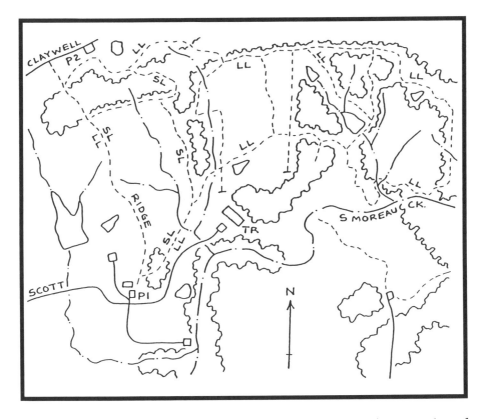

Bypass several cutoffs, staying on the Long Loop (see map) and eventually descending past an old farm pond. Trails to your left have been closed due to development of a target range (TR). Ford a stream, cross a low ridge and join the Short Loop (SL). Turn left, cross another creek and climb back to lot P1. Your excursion has totalled 5.75 miles.

30 RUNGE CONSERVATION NATURE CENTER

DISTANCE: 2 MILES
TERRAIN: HILLY
DIFFICULTY: MODERATE
WALKING TIME: 1.5 HRS.

Named for **G. Andy Runge**, a dedicated conservationist and political activist, and managed by the Missouri Department of Conservation, the **Runge Conservation Nature Center** sprawls across 112 acres on the west side of Jefferson City. Five manicured trails provide access to the preserve's hilly terrain which encompasses the varied habitats of Central Missouri.

The **Nature Center building** (open 8-5 Mon-Sat and 12-5 Sunday) houses refuge offices, meeting rooms, a library and natural history displays; the latter introduce visitors to the natural habitats and wildlife of our State. Educational programs are conducted here throughout the year, timed to coincide with nature's seasons.

The **Nature Center grounds** are open to the public from 6am-8pm, April through October and 6am-6pm, November through March. The entire preserve is closed on New Years Day, Thanksgiving and Christmas Day. There is currently no admission charge. Pets, hunting, jogging, bicycling, roller-blading and alcoholic beverages are not permitted on Nature Center grounds at any time.

Directions: From U.S. 50 on the west side of Jefferson City, take the Jamestown Exit (Missouri 179). Turn north on Commerce Drive and proceed .3 mile to the Nature Center, on your left.

Route: By combining sections of the Center's five trails, one can reach the preserve's varied habitats and achieve a loop hike of 2 miles.

Pick up the south arm of the **Towering Oak Trail (TOT)** at the northeast end of the parking lot. Hike northeastward through the forest and cross several streams before turning to the west. Bypass the cutoff on your right, fording two more creeks before intersecting the **Moss Rock Trace (MRT)**. Turn right on Moss Rock Trace, soon crossing two meadows and then passing beneath a line of rock cliffs; slump blocks, having broken from these cliffs, lie along the path.

Turn right on the **Raccoon Run Trail (RRT)**, which continues westward, passes a marsh-lined pond and makes several stream crossings. Angling toward the northwest, the trail crosses the lower end of a large meadow and then climbs toward the south. Take the **Raccoon Run Spur (RRS)** out for a fine view from the center of the meadow. Eastern bluebirds, dickcissels and northern bobwhites may be spotted on this restored prairie.

A trailside wetland at the Nature Center

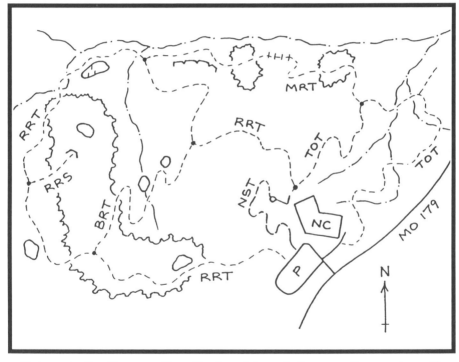

Return to the Raccoon Run Trail and turn left, ascending past another pond and then turning east to intersect the **Bluestem Ridge Trail (BRT)**. This trail snakes across the upper portion of the grassland and then re-enters the forest. After winding past two woodland ponds, the trail joins the **Raccoon Run Trail (RRT)**. Turn right, ascending toward the Nature Center building. Bypass the Towering Oak Trail, on your left and take a short stroll on the **Naturescape Trail (NST)**, which demonstrates the interdependence of plants and wildlife. This trail ends at the parking lot, completing a 2 mile loop through the Nature Center.

31 PAINTED ROCK STATE FOREST

OSAGE BLUFF SCENIC TRAIL
  DISTANCE: 1.6 MILES
  TERRAIN: HILLY
  DIFFICULTY: MODERATE
  WALKING TIME: 1.25 HRS.

CLEARCUT TRAIL
  DISTANCE: 1 MILE RT
  TERRAIN: ROLLING
  DIFFICULTY: EASY
  WALKING TIME: .75 HR.

CENTRAL TRAIL
  DISTANCE: 2 MILES RT
  TERRAIN: ROLLING, A HILL
  DIFFICULTY: EASY
  WALKING TIME: 1.25 HRS.

Sprawling above the east bank of the Osage River, **Painted Rock State Forest** boasts one of the more scenic hikes in Central Missouri. The 1490 acre preserve also harbors artifacts from native Indian tribes, which settled along the river as early as 9000 years ago. Among these artifacts are **pictographs** on the dolomite bluffs, which date from 1200-1300 AD, and an **Indian burial cairn**, constructed 500-1500 years ago.

While the **Osage Bluff Scenic Trail** is the highlight of this refuge, other trails lead to more remote sections of the forest. Resident wildlife include white-tailed deer, raccoons, wild turkey, pileated woodpeckers, turkey vultures and great horned owls. Plan a visit early or late in the day when these creatures are best observed.

Directions: From U.S. 63, 1 mile north of Westphalia, turn southwest on Missouri 133. Painted Rock's first entrance (access to the Osage Bluff Scenic Trail) will be 6.5 miles ahead, on your right.

Routes: There are 3 potential dayhikes at Painted Rock State Forest.
  Osage Bluff Scenic Trail. This 1.6 mile loop begins and ends at lot P1. An illustrated trail guide, available at the trailhead, describes highlights along the route; stations are numbered counterclockwise from the parking lot.
  Hike northwestward from the lot, winding through the forest. As the trail curves to the west, the forest begins to thin and you will soon arrive at the first observation deck, perched above the Osage River. Just before reaching this overlook you will pass the **Indian burial cairn (IBC)**, on your right (see introduction, above). The deck offers a spectacular view of the Osage Valley and of the steep dolomite cliffs that tower above the River. Turkey vultures roost on these bluffs, taking to the air by mid-morning as thermals develop along the valley wall.

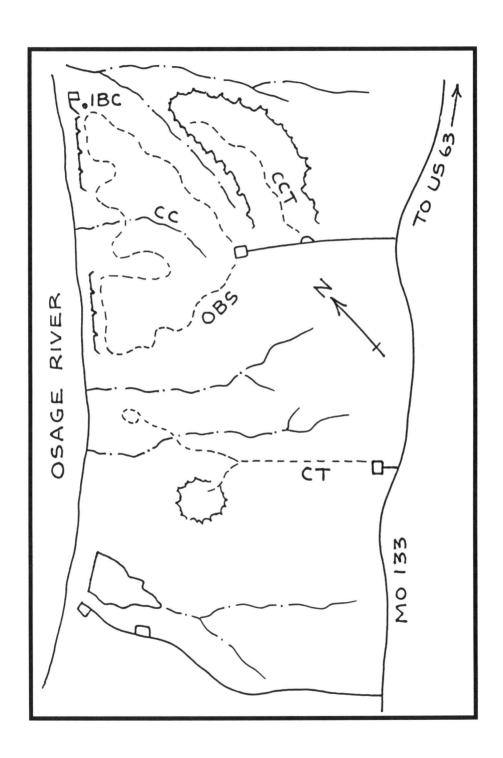

OSAGE RIVER

IBC

CC

CCT

OBS

N

CT

TO US 63

MO 133

Leaving the overlook, the trail curves southward and eastward, snaking into the scenic gorge of **Cove Creek**. Passing a rock outcrop, the path crosses the stream and then climbs the opposite wall via a long switchback. Another series of overlooks reward your effort as you turn southward above the Osage River. The trail eventually turns to the east and winds through the forest to the parking lot.

While the entire loop is moderately strenuous, less conditioned visitors can still enjoy a River view by taking either arm of the Osage Bluff Scenic Trail to the clifftop overlooks; return via the same route, thereby avoiding the steep descent and ascent through the Cove Creek gorge.

Clear Cut Trail. A .5 mile logging road (1 mile roundtrip) leaves the north side of the first entry road, .4 miles west of Route 133 (see map). The old road winds toward the northwest, passing through a clear-cut area. While not visually appealing, such areas can be excellent for wildlife watching, especially at dawn or dusk; be sure to bring your binoculars on this hike. Return via the same route.

Central Trail (CT). An old roadbed leads westward through the heart of Painted Rock State Forest, offering a peaceful escape into the woods.

Park at lot P2 off the east side of Missouri 133, .5 mile south of the first entrance. Hike eastward on the wide roadbed, following the crest of a low ridge. Within a half mile the path forks; the left fork leads out to a field. Bear right at this junction, beginning a long, gradual descent. The route ends on the valley floor where several creeks meander toward the Osage River. While this area can be "buggy" in summer, if offers a secluded picnic spot on those crisp autumn days.

Return via the same route for a roundtrip hike of 2 miles.

The Indian burial cairn

An overlook on the Osage Bluff Scenic Trail

32 BEN BRANCH LAKE CONSERVATION AREA

DOUBLE-LOOP TRAIL
    DISTANCE: 1 MILE
    TERRAIN: ROLLING
    DIFFICULTY: EASY
    WALKING TIME: .75 HR.

BACKWATER TRAIL
    DISTANCE: 2 MILES RT
    TERRAIN: HILLY
    DIFFICULTY: MODERATE
    WALKING TIME: 1.5 HRS.

Secluded in the hills of Osage County, **Ben Branch Lake** is a popular destination for fishermen. The surrounding **Conservation Area**, covering 499 acres, is a mix of forest, fields and cedar glades. Two trails provide access to this hilly terrain and yield views of the scenic lake.

Directions: From U.S. 50, three miles east of Linn, turn north on Missouri 89. Drive 9 miles and turn left (west) on Road 314. Proceed .7 miles to a road junction; bear left to access the **Backwater Trail** and the boat ramp area. Those heading to the dam area and **Double-Loop Trail** should bear right at the junction, proceed another .3 mile and turn left onto Road 313. The entry road to the dam area will be .6 mile ahead, on your left (see map).

Routes: The are two potential dayhikes at Ben Branch Lake Conservation Area; the names used are purely descriptive.

Double-Loop Trail (DL). This hike, which begins and ends at the dam parking lot, covers 1 mile. Before taking the loop hike, you may want to stroll onto the dam for a fine view of Ben Branch Lake.

Pick up the trail that descends southward, just west of the restroom hut. Turn left at the pond, descending further to the valley floor. Continue southwestward along the edge of the valley meadow until the trail curves northward to parallel the lake's outlet stream.

Complete the valley loop, ascend to the pond and hike northwestward on an old road bed that cuts through the woodland between the pond and the entry road. Exiting these woods, turn right and return to the parking area via the entry road which offers broad views of the lake and surrounding uplands.

Backwater Trail (BWT). This trail, covering 2 miles roundtrip, offers the best dayhike at Ben Branch Lake; it begins on the east side of the boat ramp road, just south of Road 314 (see map).

Hike eastward through the woods on this wide path which soon angles to the southeast and gradually descends toward an inlet of the lake. Once in the valley, it enters a field. Proceed to the north end of the field and pick up the trail as it re-enters the woodland, crosses the inlet stream and climbs eastward through the forest.

Ben Branch Lake

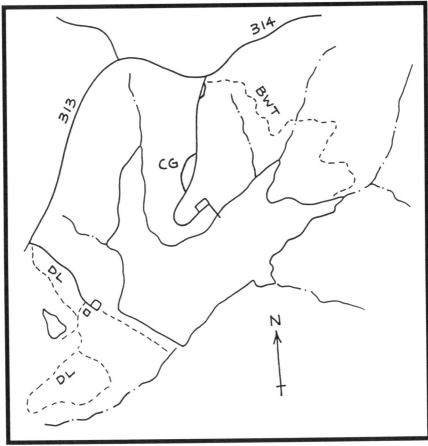

Curving southward, the path yields a view of Ben Branch Lake and then begins a winding descent to a second inlet area. Turn right and hike through the field and open woodlands to the backwater shore. Return to your car via the same route.

33 BIG BUFFALO CREEK C.A.

LONG LOOP HIKE
  DISTANCE: 3.5 MILES
  TERRAIN: HILLY
  DIFFICULTY: MODERATE
  WALKING TIME: 2 HRS.

SHORT LOOP HIKE
  DISTANCE: 1.6 MILES
  TERRAIN: HILLY
  DIFFICULTY: MODERATE
  WALKING TIME: 1 HR.

This remote Conservation Area, which stretches across the north wall of the **Big Buffalo Creek** valley, offers one of the best loop hikes in central Missouri. A rich, hardwood forest, heavily dissected terrain and a secluded back-country lake characterize the preserve which is home to an excellent diversity of wildlife. Hikers are likely to encounter white-tailed deer, wild turkeys, pileated woodpeckers and ruffed grouse along the trails.

Directions: From Missouri 52, 1.5 miles west of Stover, turn south on Route FF. Proceed 8 miles and turn right (west) on Big Buffalo Road, immediately crossing a fork of the creek. The trailhead for the Short Loop will be .7 mile ahead (see map) while the Long Loop trailhead will be another .35 mile (just over 1 mile from FF).

Routes: There are two primary loop hikes at Big Buffalo Creek Conservation Area; we refer to them as the Short and Long Loops.
  Long Loop Hike (LL). From the trailhead lot, on Big Buffalo Road, hike northward on a trail that begins just beyond the shed (S). After two quick stream crossings the trail begins a long, steady climb through the forest. Once atop the ridge, the path angles to the northwest and soon skirts the edge of a meadow. Re-entering the forest, the trail curves back to the south and reaches a junction; turn right on this old jeep road for a short hike down to a secluded, woodland lake (see map).
  After rest and refreshment at the lake, hike back up to the junction and continue southward on the old jeep road. This wide path follows high ground for almost a mile before making a steady descent to the Area's campground (CG). Hike out to Big Buffalo Road, turn left and return to your car, completing a loop hike of 3.5 miles.

  Short Loop Hike (SL). From its trailhead lot (see map), this 1.6 mile loop trail leads northward into the forest, crossing and recrossing a stream within a short distance. Wildflowers are abundant in this creek valley during the spring and early summer.
  Within a quarter mile the trail makes a sharp turn to the right and climbs away from the stream; this short but steep climb curves to the southeast before the path levels out and angles northeastward. A final curve and short descent bring you back to the roadway. Turn right and hike back to the trailhead lot.

This secluded lake is accessed via the Long Loop

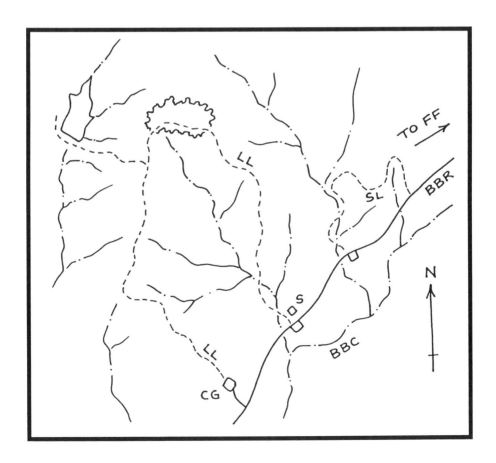

34 SALINE VALLEY CONSERVATION AREA

DISTANCE: DAYHIKES OF 2-3.6 MILES
TERRAIN: ROLLING TO HILLY
DIFFICULTY: EASY TO MODERATE
WALKING TIME: 1.5-2.5 HRS.

Draped across the valleys of Saline Creek, Little Saline Creek and the Osage River, this 4783 acre Conservation Area offers a number of excellent dayhikes. Since stream crossings are impossible during much of the year, we suggest the routes described below. On the other hand, the sandy channel and gravel bars of Saline Creek provide another unique hiking opportunity during the dry season.

Directions: The Saline Valley Conservation Area is approximately 4 miles southeast of Eldon or 1.2 miles northeast of Tuscumbia.
   To reach trailhead **lots P1, P2 and P3** (see map), turn southeast on Route M from U.S. 54 in Eldon. The refuge boundary will be 3.8 miles ahead. Drive another 4 miles to the junction of Saline and Woods Roads (just past the campground) and bear right on Woods Road. Proceed to the lots as illustrated.
   To reach the **Jim Henry Road trailhead lot (P4)**, turn south on Route 17 from U.S. 54 (near Eugene). Drive 7.2 miles to Jim Henry Road, on your left; the trailhead lot will be at this junction, on the east side of Route 17 (see map).
   To reach **lot P5, access to the Osage Valley Loop**, head northeast on Route 17 from its junction with Missouri 52 in Tuscumbia. The lot will be 1.2 miles ahead, on your left.

Routes: The following dayhikes provide an overview of the topography and natural habitats found at the Saline Valley Conservation Area. The trail names are purely descriptive.
   Saline Ridge Trail (SRT). This 1 mile trail (2 miles roundtrip) begins and ends at lot P1, at the crest of a hill on Woods Road, .3 mile south of its junction with Saline Road. Cross the road and hike eastward and then southeastward atop the ridge. Within a half mile you will cross a power line swath which provides a sweeping view to the west. Beyond this clearing the trail re-enters the forest, parallels the power line to the east and then turns southeast, snaking above several drainages. The trail currently ends in this ridgetop forest but, we suspect, may eventually connect with the Saline Valley Trail (next hike). Return to your car via the same route.

118

Saline Creek

The Jim Henry Ridge Trail

Little Saline Valley Trail (LSVT). This hike, 2 miles roundtrip, begins and ends at lot P2 on Woods Road, .5 mile south of the junction with Saline Road. Follow a wide path that heads east from the lot, hugging the edge of the valley floor. Since this trail follows the border between the hillside forest and the valley meadows, it is an excellent route for birdwatching. Shallow wetlands are also spaced along trail which ends in bottomland timber near the confluence of Little Saline and Saline Creeks. Return via the same route.

Church Ridge Trail (CRT). This hike begins and ends at lot P3, next to a church on Woods Road, .8 miles southwest of the junction with Saline Road. Hike northwestward on a wide path and turn right at the first trail intersection, crossing a stream. Bear left at the next junction, fording the creek once again. Stay on the main trail which climbs to the northwest; one mile from the trailhead you will reach a ridgetop clearing, an excellent spot for a picnic lunch. Return via the same route for a roundtrip hike of 2 miles.

Jim Henry Ridge Trail (JHR). This moderately strenuous hike begins and ends at the trailhead lot (P4) at the junction of Jim Henry Road and Route 17 (see map and directions). Covering 3.6 miles, roundtrip, it offers some fine views of the surrounding countryside.

Hike southward on an old jeep road which follows the crest of the ridge and soon crosses a powerline swath; this yields a broad view to the west. Continuing southward you will soon be treated to views of the Osage River Valley before reaching the site of an old homestead (H). Bear right at the fork in the trail and begin a long, gradual descent to the east bank of Saline Creek; the Missouri 17 bridge can be seen to the northwest. After rest and refreshment along the Creek, return via the same route.

Osage Valley Loop (OVL). For a 3.6 mile excursion across the north wall of the Osage River Valley, begin at lot P5, on Route 17, 1.2 miles northeast of Tuscumbia (see map and directions). Hike northward from the lot, passing an old cemetery (C) on your left. After crossing two small streams, the trail begins a steady climb onto the forested ridge which separates the Osage and Little Saline Creek valleys. Once atop the ridge, the trail angles to the northeast for a pleasant stroll across high ground.

Bypass the cutoff, on your right, which leads down to lot P6, and continue eastward. The trail soon crosses a meadow and then climbs a bit higher, entering an open forest with large trees. This scenic hilltop yields a sweeping view (V) to the north.

Return to the trail intersection and turn left (south), descending toward lot P6. Complete the loop by hiking southwestward along Missouri 17; lot P5 will be .6 mile ahead.

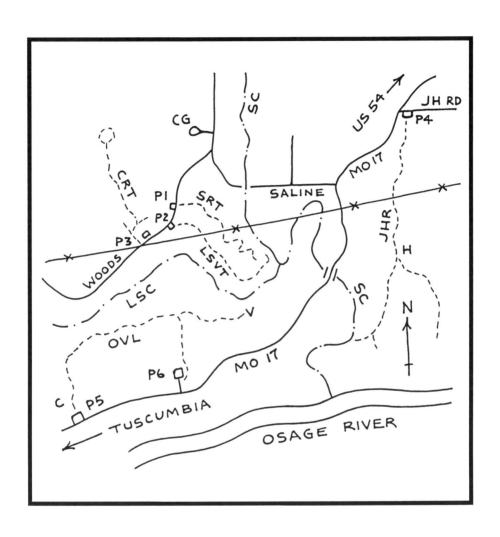

121

35 SPRING CREEK GAP CONSERVATION AREA

DISTANCE: 3-3.5 MILES ROUNDTRIP
TERRAIN: ROLLING TO HILLY
DIFFICULTY: EASY TO MODERATE
WALKING TIME: 2-2.5 HRS.

Perched above the east wall of the Gasconade River Valley, **Spring Creek Gap Conservation Area** covers 1816 acres in Maries County. The rugged Cedar Creek gorge, which bisects the refuge, harbors some of the most scenic landscape in Central Missouri. While a mature forest of oak and hickory cloaks most of the preserve, Spring Creek Gap is well known to naturalists for its large number of glades; these natural clearings, where dolomite outcrops and thin soil retard forest invasion, are home to native prairie flora.

Directions: From U.S. 63, approximately 2 miles northwest of Vichy (.8 miles west of the Route 28 junction) turn north on Old 63; this road is just across U.S. 63 from a scenic overlook. Drive 1.2 miles to the trailhead lot which is on the north side of the road, across from the Vichy Lookout Tower (T).

Routes: Two main trails, which we call the Ridge and Creek Trails, provide access to the refuge. A number of smaller trails interconnect with these primary routes.
   Ridge Trail (RT). An old jeep trail leads northward from the trailhead lot, following the crest of the ridge for most of its route. Bypass cutoffs to your right and left, including the Creek Trail (CT), which drops to the floor of the Cedar Creek Gorge. The forest opens up near the north end of the ridge, yielding views to the northwest. This is a good turn-around point since the trail begins to narrow and merely snakes down to County Road 323. Return via the same route for a roundtrip hike of 3 miles.

   Creek Trail (CT). Adventurous and conditioned hikers may want to hike down to Cedar Creek, enjoying spectacular views of the central gorge along the way. From the trailhead, hike northward on the Ridge Trail for 1 mile, bypassing cutoffs on either side. Bear right onto the Creek Trail (CT); this junction is a short distance before the Ridge Trail reaches a small pond (see map).
   Follow the Creek Trail as it snakes into the gorge via broad switchbacks which yield magnificent views of the forested slopes that ring the valley; the gorge is especially scenic in October, when autumn colors paint the woodland.
   While the Creek Trail continues southeastward, climbing onto the east wall of the gorge, it does not connect with other routes. We thus suggest turning back from the valley floor for a roundtrip hike of 3.5 miles.

122

The Cedar Creek Gorge

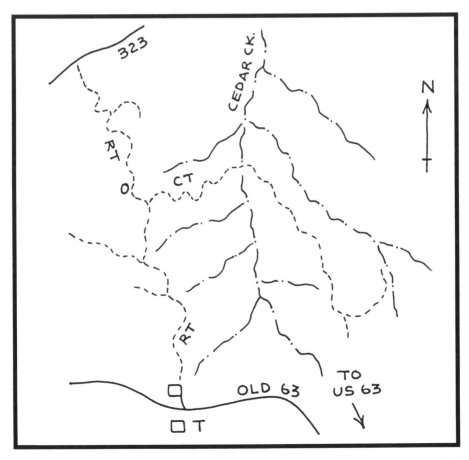

36 CANAAN CONSERVATION AREA

DISTANCE: DAYHIKES OF 1.5-4 MILES
TERRAIN: HILLY
DIFFICULTY: MODERATE
WALKING TIME: 1-3 HRS.

Spreading south from Sulphur Branch Creek, in Gasconade County, the 1435 acres of **Canaan Conservation Area** occupy the land of two working farms that were settled by German Immigrants in the mid 1800s. Some crop fields are still maintained for wildlife though much of the preserve is covered by forest and open woodlands. Access is provided by old farm roads and field trails.

Directions: From Missouri 28 in Bland, turn north on Route A.

Rehmert Road will be .9 mile north of Bland. Turn right (east) here and drive 3.1 miles to reach lot P5.

Road A2 280 will be 1.3 miles north of Bland. Turn right (east) here to reach lots P1 and P2 (see map).

Boettcher Road will be 3.1 miles north of Bland. Turn right (east) here to reach lots P3 and P4 (see map).

Routes: We suggest the following dayhikes. Trail names are purely descriptive.

Central Trail (CT). This 2 mile trail (4 miles RT) runs between lots P1 and P3; much of the route uses an old farm road. From lot P1, hike to the north on a wide field trail; within 1/4 mile, the path forks. Turn right and descend into a creek valley where a trail from lot P2 comes in from the south.

Turn northward, hiking along the edge of a field and paralleling the stream. The trail soon crosses this creek and then climbs gradually through open woods, fording several sidestreams. A short but steep climb through the forest brings you to the edge of another field. Turn right here, staying on the main path as it passes along and through a series of meadows. Once past a large, marsh-lined pond, on your right, the trail re-enters the woods and begins a gradual .5 mile descent to lot P4. Return via the same route for a roundtrip hike of 4 miles.

East Trail (ET). This .75 mile trail (1.5 miles roundtrip) is a short but steep route between lots P4 and P5; the elevation gain from P4 to P5 is 200 feet. From lot P4, the trail follows an arm of Sulphur Branch Creek toward the southeast. It soon crosses this stream and continues eastward through a rocky channel. Watch for a cutoff on your right where the trail begins a winding ascent to lot P5 and Rehmert Road which command a broad view to the south. Return to lot P4 via the same route.

A ridgetop meadow at Canaan

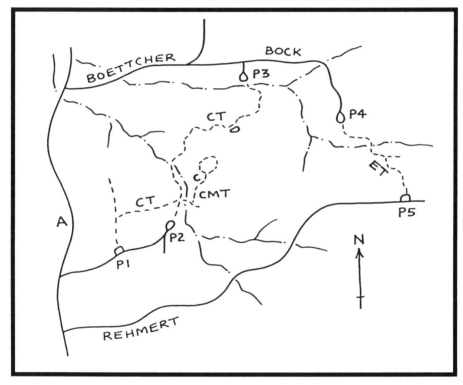

Cemetery Trail (CMT). This 2 mile hike begins and ends at lot P2. Hike northeastward on a wide path to a clearing where several trails intersect (see map). Cross the creek and turn left at the next junction, hiking northward along the edge of a field. The trail soon climbs into the forest via an old jeep road; leveling out atop the ridge, the road leads to the **Old Bland Methodist-Episcopal Cemetery (C)**, founded in 1868.

Past the cemetery, a tractor swath circles a large field, hugging the treeline. Complete this loop and then return to lot P2 via your entry route.

37 LAKE OF THE OZARKS STATE PARK

DISTANCE: DAYHIKES OF .5 TO 8 MILES
TERRAIN: HILLY
DIFFICULTY: EASY TO MODERATE
WALKING TIME: .5 TO 5.5 HRS.

Renowned as a destination for boaters and fishermen, Missouri's Lake of the Ozarks also offers excellent hiking opportunities. Indeed, **Lake of the Ozarks State Park**, tucked away in the forested hills that line the Lake's Grand Glaize arm, provides a peaceful escape from the congestion of the U.S. 54 corridor.

Covering more than 17,000 acres, this is Missouri's largest State Park. A rich hardwood forest, sheer rock cliffs, caves, springs, fens, prairie plots and numerous streams characterize this diverse refuge which attracts naturalists and outdoor adventurers throughout the year.

Directions: Most of the hiking trails begin along Route 134 which cuts south from Missouri 42, 3.5 miles east of U.S. 54 (at Osage Beach). Proceed to parking lots as illustrated on the overview map (next page).

Access to the Rocky Top Trail is on the east side of U.S. 54, 4.4 miles south of the Missouri 42 junction. Take the Grand Glaize Beach Road, eventually bearing right, toward the Picnic Area (lot P7)

Access to the Grand Glaize Trail is via Route A which leads eastward from U.S. 54, 10.5 miles south of the Missouri 42 junction. Drive 6.9 miles on Route A and turn left (north) on McCubbins Dr. Proceed another 2.4 miles to the trailhead lot (P8).

The Ozark Caverns and the Coakley Hollow Trail are also reached via Route A. Proceed east for 6.9 miles to McCubbins Dr., turn left (north) and watch for the graveled road to Ozark Caverns, on your right.

*One of many
lake views
at the Park*

Winter offers solitude and vistas

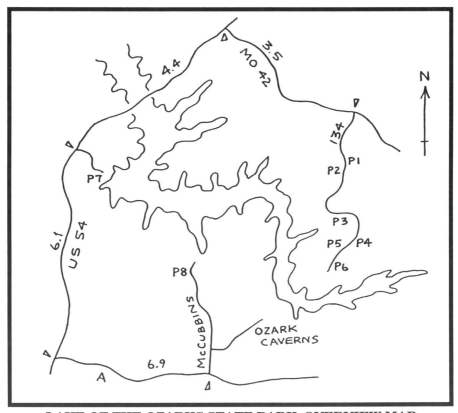

LAKE OF THE OZARKS STATE PARK: OVERVIEW MAP

Routes: As mentioned above, most of the trails at Lake of the Ozarks State Park are accessed via Route 134, off Missouri 42 (per directions). Trailhead lots P1-P6 (our designation) service these routes.

Bluestem Knoll Savanna (BKS). A .5 mile loop trail begins and ends at lot P1, 1 mile south of Missouri 42. This trail circles a glade area where prairie flora and fauna may be observed; see map next page.

Lazy Hollow Trail (LHT). Blazed with green arrows, this .5 mile loop begins and ends across Route 134 from lot P2. The route circles through a forested stream valley; see map next page.

Woodland Trail. Providing access to the Patterson Hollow Wild Area, this double-loop trail, blazed with blue arrows (BT), covers 6 miles; by using the Orange Connector Trail (OCT), the loop is cut to 2 miles; by using the Yellow Connector Trail (YCT), the loop is cut to 4.2 miles. The entrance trail is just northwest of lot P2.
Designated a State Wild Area, **Patterson Hollow** is cloaked by a rich, oak-hickory forest. Pileated woodpeckers and wild turkey are common in these woods and the streams are home to southern redbelly dace, orange-throated darters and creek chub. The trail's route is illustrated below.

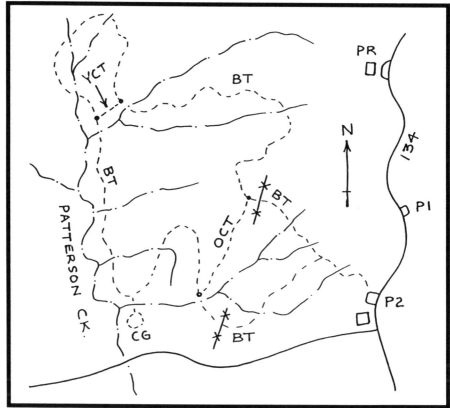

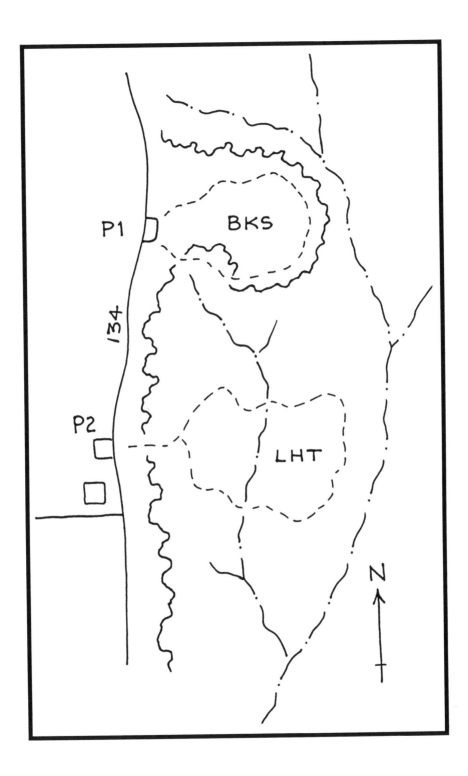

P1

134

P2

BKS

LHT

N

Trail of Four Winds. This trail complex is accessed from lots P3 and P4 (see map). Its segments are blazed with **blue (TWB)**, **white (TWW)**, **yellow (TWY)** and **red (TWR)**. We suggest the following dayhikes:

White Trail to Overlook. The **White Trail** is an old jeep road that leads southwest from lot P3. Follow this path until it splits into the Blue and Red Trails (see map). Bear left (straight) onto the **Red Trail**, cross a stream and climb to the overlook cutoff, on your right. The **overlook deck (V)** yields a broad view of the forested valley. Return to lot P3 via the same route for a roundtrip hike of 2.4 miles.

Blue-Red-Yellow Loop. Start at lot P3, hike southwestward on the White Trail for a short distance and turn right on the **Blue Trail**. At the junction with the Red Trail, turn left, staying on the Blue Trail. You will soon cross a drainage and then wind to the west. Bypass a cutoff on your left, staying on the main trail which eventually curves southward above an arm of the Lake. At the next junction, turn right onto the **Red Trail** which crosses a creek and climbs to the **Overlook (V)** cutoff. After taking in the view, continue southeastward on the Red Trail, cross a powerline swath and turn left at the junction with the **Yellow Trail**. This 2-mile segment leads eastward and then northward, crossing several streams along the way; it eventually intersects the White Trail. Turn right and return to lot P3, completing a 4.5 mile loop.

Red Trail Loop. Conditioned hikers may want to complete the entire Red Trail loop, which covers 8 miles. The route can be accessed from lot P3 by using either segment of the White Trail (TWW) but is perhaps best hiked from lot P4; the Red Trail crosses the Park road just north of this lot (see map). Note: older maps may not show the segment of the Red Trail east of the Park roadway; this extension, which snakes around the Airport, was a recent addition to the Trail of Four Winds.

The Overlook;
Trail of
Four Winds

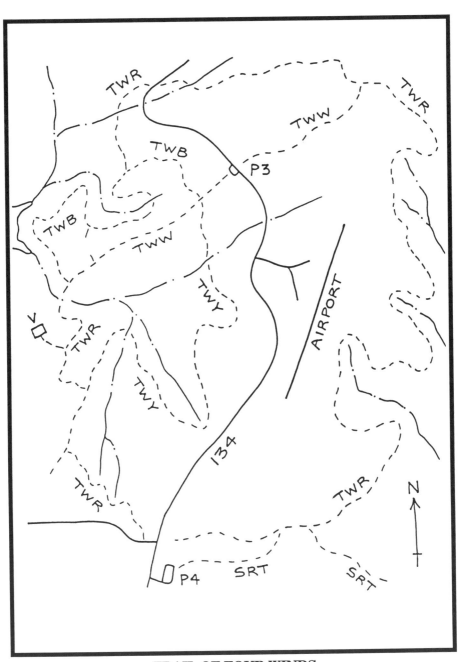

TRAIL OF FOUR WINDS
RED-TWR   BLUE-TWB   WHITE-TWW   YELLOW-TWY

Squaw's Revenge Trail (SRT). Perhaps the best loop hike in the State Park, this 2-mile trail, blazed with green arrows, begins and ends at lot P4. Pick up the southernmost arm which leads eastward through the forest and eventually descends to cross a network of streams. It follows the last of these toward the south before climbing away to the east and passing the **cemetery (C)** from an 1860's homestead.

It then curves northward to cross another drainage and then climbs to the east to reach a series of **overlooks (V)** above the Lake of the Ozarks. A small island in the Lake adds to the scenic beauty. Once beyond the cliffs and overlooks, the trail angles to the northwest and soon intersects the **Red segment of the Trail of Four Winds** (see pages 130-131). Bear left, staying on the Squaw's Revenge Trail which crosses a stream and then leads westward to lot P4.

Fawn's Ridge Trail (FRT). This 2.5 mile, double-loop hike begins and ends at lot P5. Cross the park road and hike along a paved path that winds down to a trail junction and then leads southwestward for .5 mile to the campground entrance. Turn left, descending into the forest on an earthen trail and soon reaching a junction; the 1 mile **Lake View Bend Trail (LVT)** leads off to the right, running above the lake and ending at the tip of the campgrounds peninsula.

Turn left at this junction, staying on the Fawn's Ridge Trail and gradually climbing through a stream valley. Nearing the upper reaches of this drainage, the trail intersects another path; this is the second loop of the Fawn's Ridge Trail, blazed with blue arrows. Turn right, cross several creeks and then complete a ridgetop loop (see map). Backtrack to the paved entry trail and return to lot P5.

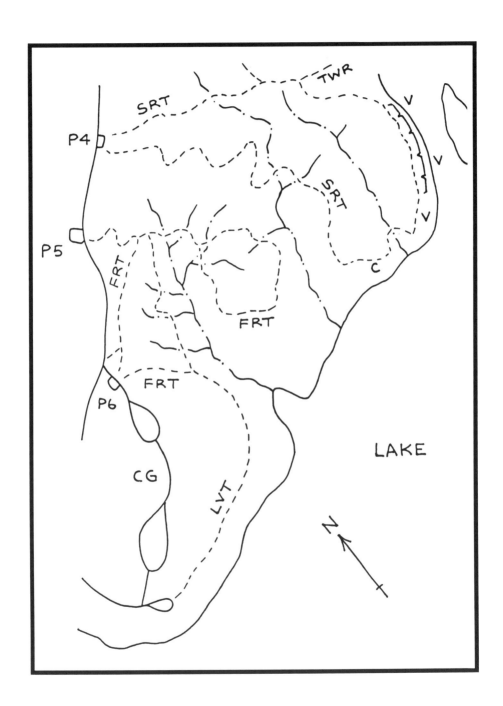

LAKE

133

Rocky Top Trail (RTT). This 3-mile, double-loop hike begins and ends at the Picnic Area just south of Grand Glaize Beach (lot P7). Pick up the trail on the west side of the picnic grounds loop and climb into the woods. You will soon cross a broad clearing where outcrops of dolomite retard forest invasion. At the west end of this glade the trail re-enters the forest and begins a gradual descent into a stream valley. Nearing the creek, you will reach a trail intersection; turn right, cross the stream and complete the southern loop of the Rocky Top Trail. The east end of this loop offers sweeping views of the Lake.

After completing the southern loop, re-cross the central creek and turn right at the intersection. The trail leads eastward above the stream which soon enters an inlet of the Lake. Arriving at the end of the peninsula, you can climb back to the picnic grounds via a number of paths (see map on next page).

Grand Glaize Trail (GGT). Blazed with yellow arrows, this 2.5 mile loop hike begins and ends at lot P8 (see Directions). After entering the woods, the trail crosses a powerline swath and soon forks. Bear right at this junction, beginning a long, gradual descent to the northwest and crossing a number of drainages along the way (see map, below).

The trail eventually crosses the main stream channel and then climbs through a cedar glade. Angling to the southeast, the path follows high ground between two creek valleys. After crossing the upper drainages of one of these streams, the trail intersects your entry route. Turn right and return to lot P8.

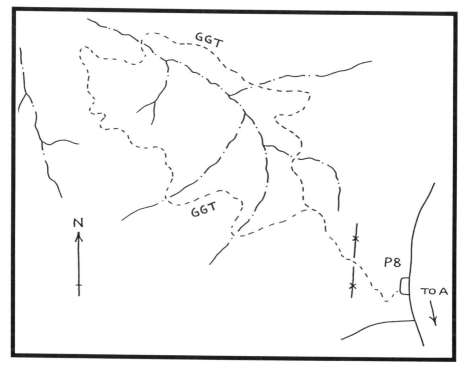

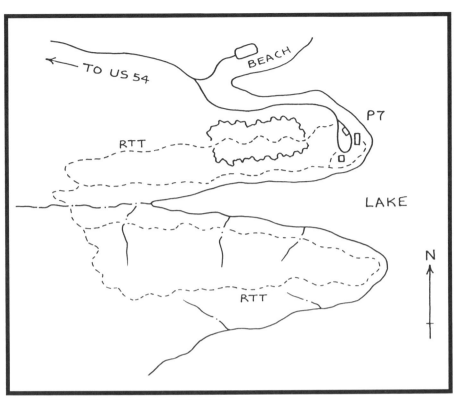

TO US 54

BEACH

P7

RTT

LAKE

N

RTT

Scene along the Rocky Top Trail

135

38 HA HA TONKA STATE PARK

QUARRY TRAIL
  DISTANCE: 2 MILES
  TERRAIN: HILLY
  DIFFICULTY: MODERATE
  WALKING TIME: 1.5 HRS.

SCENIC LOOP
  DISTANCE: 4.5-6.0 MILES
  TERRAIN: HILLY
  DIFFICULTY: STRENUOUS
  WALKING TIME: 3-4 HRS.

TURKEY PEN HOLLOW TRAIL
  DISTANCE: 5 MILES
  TERRAIN: HILLY
  DIFFICULTY: MODERATE
  WALKING TIME: 3.5 HRS.

Rich in geologic features, human history and scenic beauty, **Ha Ha Tonka State Park** offers some of the best hiking in Central Missouri. The Park is renowned for its karst topography---springs, caves, sinkholes and natural bridges---which have resulted from water erosion of the region's thick dolomite formation. This rock, deposited in shallow seas of the Ordovician Period, forms spectacular bluffs above the Lake of the Ozarks, which borders the west side of the Park.

Ha Ha Tonka also harbors open savannas and dolomite glades where sunny, dry conditons favor the growth of oak woodlands and ridgetop prairies. The latter are home to prairie scorpions, Missouri tarantulas and numerous wildflowers. Of historic interest are the ruins of Robert Snyder's mansion; a Kansas City businessman, Snyder began construction of his clifftop castle in 1905. Following his death a year later, Snyder's family completed the mansion which eventually served as a hotel. Unfortunately, the structure was destroyed by fire in 1942.

Directions: From U.S. 54, approximately 1 mile south of Camdenton, turn east on Route D. Ha Ha Tonka's Visitor Center will be 1.5 miles ahead. Proceed to lots as illustrated on the map.

Lot P1 provides access to the castle ruins and to the Quarry Trail (QT). Lot P2, near the Park's Natural Bridge (NB), is the entry point for the Colosseum Trail (CT). Lot P3 serves the Acorn Trail (AT), Turkey Pen Hollow Trail (TPH and the Devil's Kitchen Trail (DKT); the latter is also reached from lot P5. Both lots P4 and P6 provide access to the Spring Trail (ST) and Island Trail. Lot P6 should be used for hiking the Boulder Ridge Trail (BRT).

The castle ruins overlook the Ha Ha Tonka gorge

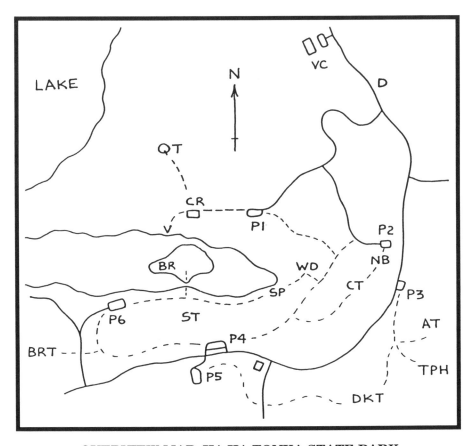

OVERVIEW MAP: HA HA TONKA STATE PARK

Routes: There are many potential dayhikes at Ha Ha Tonka State Park. We suggest three loop hikes, described below. Due to the hilly terrain, all three are of moderate-strenuous difficulty. Those preferring short, easy hikes should consider the following:

>   **Lot P1 to Castle Ruins and Overlook** - .5 mile roundtrip
>   **Lot P6 to Ha Ha Tonka Spring (SP)** - 1 mile roundtrip

Quarry Trail (QT). This 2 mile loop hike begins and ends at lot P1. Hike westward on the paved path to the **castle ruins (CR)** and out to an **overlook (V)** of the Springs Gorge, 250 feet above the surface of the Lake. After enjoying the view, pick up the **Quarry Trail**, blazed with green arrows. Bear left at the junction, winding to the west and descending toward the boat dock; just after skirting the edge of an old quarry, turn right at the trail intersection (see map). The Quarry Trail leads northward, crosses a stream and soon runs below a rock outcrop. Climbing onto the ridge, it enters a cedar grove and intersects the **White Connector Trail (WCT).**

Turn left here for an excursion above the Lake of the Ozarks; crossing through open glades, you are treated to continuous views to the west. The trail eventually curves to the right and climbs through a rocky outcrop. Turning southward, the path leads through more ridgetop glades and soon intersects the White Connector Trail once again. Bear left, hiking eastward through a rich forest before curving south to enter an **old quarry site (Q)**. Once through the quarry, the trail crosses a stream and then leads back to lot P1.

Scenic Loop. This strenuous, 4.5 mile loop, begins and ends at lot P2. It combines sections of several trails and leads past some of the Park's more scenic geologic features.

From lot P2, hike southward, skirting the edge of a sinkhole. The **Colosseum Trail (CT)** passes under the **Natural Bridge (NB)** and then climbs along the wall of the **Colosseum** itself, a large sinkhole that was formed by the collapse of a cave. Continue westward beneath towering walls of rock and turn right at the intersection with the **Spring Trail (ST)**. Crossing the wall of the Ha Ha Tonka Spring gorge, you are soon treated to a spectacular view of the castle ruins sitting above sheer cliffs of dolomite.

Turn left on the stairway (see map), descending past **Whispering Dell (WD)**, another sinkhole, and eventually reaching the floor of the gorge where **Ha Ha Tonka Spring (SP)** discharges 48 million gallons of water a day into this scenic inlet of Lake of the Ozarks. Hike westward along the inlet and cross onto the **Island** which is accessed by a .75 mile loop trail; **Balanced Rock (BR)** will be found near the western end of the circuit.

Return to the **Spring Trail (ST)** and continue westward. Nearing lot P6, the trail cuts to the left and climbs through the forest. Those wanting to include the **Boulder Ridge Trail (BRT)**, a 1.5 mile loop, should watch

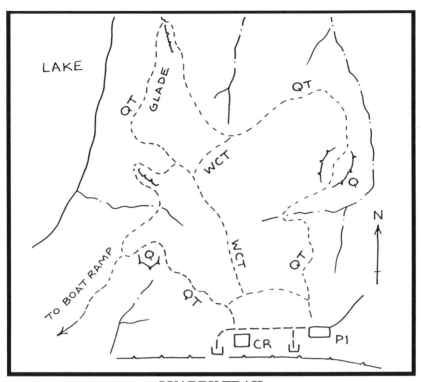

QUARRY TRAIL

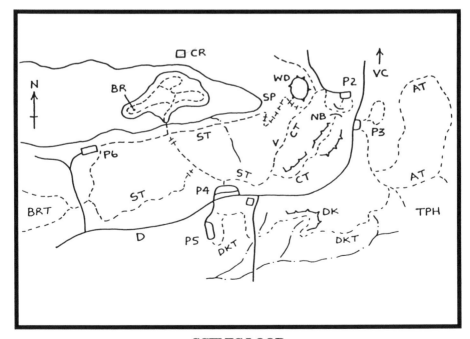

SCENIC LOOP

for its junction, on the right. The **Spring Trail** leaves the woodland and crosses an open, rocky area as it curves back to the east. Re-entering the forest, the trail joins up with the **White Connector (WC)** and continues on to lot P4, accessed by a short stairway.

From lot P4, cross the roadway and pick up the **Devil's Kitchen Trail (DKT)** via one of several entry points (see map). This trail leads eastward through the forest and then turn south along Road D-144. After crossing this road, the path negotiates a few drainages and soon arrives at **Devil's Kitchen (DK)**, formed by a collapsed cave system. The trail hugs the edge of this sink as it circles to the east and south before climbing eastward through a stream valley. Turning to the north, the path leaves the forest and intersects the **Acorn** and **Turkey Pen Hollow Trails**. Turn right and follow the **Acorn Trail (AT)** as it circles a forested knob, passing through an open, oak savanna. Thin, rocky soil in this area favors the growth of prairie grasses, wildflowers and drought-tolerant woodlands; the latter include post, black and blackjack oaks.

Complete the Acorn Trail Loop, descend to lot P3 and cross the roadway. Hike atop the **Natural Bridge (NB)** and return to lot P2 (see map).

Turkey Pen Hollow Trail (TPH). This 5 mile back-country loop (formerly 7 miles in length) is accessed from lot P3. Climb southward on the common entry path for the Acorn, Devil's Kitchen and Turkey Pen Hollow Trails (see map).

Blazed red, the trail loop can be hiked in either direction; the map on page 141 illustrates its route. As indicated above, the trail used to cover 7 miles; the southeastern end has now been closed and a **White Connector Trail (WCT)** completes the 5 mile loop.

Hikers will appreciate the fact that most of the route follows high ground; nevertheless, elevations range from 780 to 1080 feet and a few steep climbs/descents, especially near stream crossings, will be encountered. Back-country camping is permitted in the area but those planning overnight trips must register at the park office.

The oak savanna

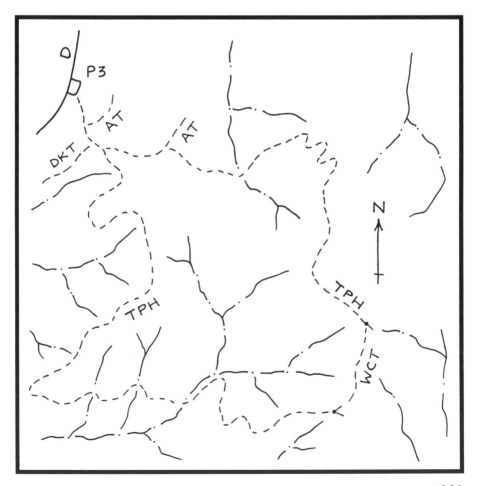

39 LEAD MINE CONSERVATION AREA

VALLEY TRAIL
  DISTANCE: 4 MILES RT
  TERRAIN: ROLLING
  DIFFICULTY: MODERATE
  WALKING TIME: 2.5 HRS.

GREEN-BLUE LOOP
  DISTANCE: 5 MILES
  TERRAIN: HILLY
  DIFFICULTY: STRENUOUS
  WALKING TIME: 3.5 HRS.

ORANGE TRAIL LOOP
  DISTANCE: 3.2 MILES
  TERRAIN: HILLY
  DIFFICULTY: MODERATE
  WALKING TIME: 2 HRS.

A popular destination for horsemen, the 7180 acres of **Lead Mine Conservation Area** are draped across a ridge on the west side of the Niangua River Valley. Upland oak-hickory forest, dolomite glades and valley meadows characterize the preserve which is accessed by graveled roads and an extensive network of bridal paths. Jakes Creek runs through the eastern side of the refuge, enhancing the scenic beauty of this remote area.

Though small lead mines once operated in the area, the Conservation Area is named for the town of Lead Mine, a Mennonite farming community just west of the preserve.

Directions: From U.S. 54, 2.5 miles southwest of Mack's Creek, turn south on Route 73. Drive 6.2 miles to Tunas and turn left (east) on Route E. Proceed 3.8 miles to the town of Lead Mine and turn right (south) on Route T. Drive .7 mile to Route YY; turn left (east) and proceed another .5 mile to the entrance, on your left. We have numbered the parking lots for the purposes of this guide.

Routes: The vast network of bridal paths offers a variety of potential dayhikes. In addition, a .5 mile **Nature Trail (NT)** circles a short ridge above the Niangua River (see map). We suggest the following routes; trail names are purely descriptive.

Valley Trail (VT). This 4 mile (roundtrip) hike begins and ends at lot P2 (see map). Follow the trail northward from the lot, bearing left at the fork. The trail descends into a creek valley where it reaches a trail junction; turn right here, hiking downstream and soon crossing through a small valley meadow. The trail crosses the stream, re-enters the forest and intersects the **Orange Horse Trail (OT)**. Continue eastward through the valley, crossing several sidestreams and bypassing cutoffs that climb to the north. The Valley Trail eventually enters a large meadow where Jake's Creek and a gravel road come in from the south. After rest and refreshment along the creek, return to lot P2 via the same route.

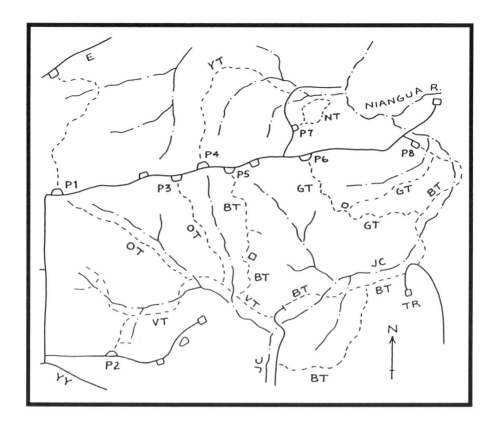

Green-Blue Loop. Park at lot P6 and hike southeastward through the forest on the **Green Horse Trail (GT)**. Bear right (straight) at the fork, descending into the Jake's Creek Valley. You will intersect the **Blue Horse Trail (BT)** on the valley floor; turn right, ford Jake's Creek and cross north of the target range (TR), using a section of the roadway (see map). Continue westward on the Blue Trail, bypassing a cutoff on your left. The trail crosses Jake's Creek once again, runs through a large field and reaches another gravel road. Stay on the Blue Trail as it angles to the northwest, crosses a valley meadow and then enters the woods. The Blue Trail then turns away to the north (see map), climbing out of the valley and soon passing an old homestead. Bear left at the trail junction, continuing out to lot P5. Turn right on the gravel road and hike another .6 mile to lot P6, completing a loop hike of 5 miles.

Orange Trail Loop. This 3.2 mile loop uses a section of the **Orange Horse Trail (OT)**. Park at lot P1, cross the road and pick up the Orange Trail as it descends to the southeast along a stream. Once on the floor of the valley, turn left at the junction, crossing the creek that you have been following. Hike another quarter mile and turn left on the Orange Trail as it climbs to the north. This route leads out to lot P3; turn left on the road and hike 1.2 miles back to lot P1.

40 BENNETT SPRING STATE PARK

NATURE CENTER LOOP
  DISTANCE: 1.5 MILES
  TERRAIN: HILLY
  DIFFICULTY: MODERATE
  WALKING TIME: .75 HR.

SPRING TRAIL
  DISTANCE: 1.4 MILES RT
  TERRAIN: FLAT
  DIFFICULTY: EASY
  WALKING TIME: .75 HR.

SAVANNA RIDGE TRAIL
  DISTANCE: 2.5 MILES
  TERRAIN: HILLY
  DIFFICULTY: MODERATE
  WALKING TIME: 1.5 HRS.

NATURAL TUNNEL TRAIL
  DISTANCE: 7.5 MILES
  TERRAIN: ROLLING
  DIFFICULTY: MODERATE
  WALKING TIME: 4.5 HRS.

A mecca for fly-fishermen, **Bennett Spring State Park** stretches along the valley of Missouri's third-largest spring. Gushing 100 million gallons of water each day, Bennett Spring feeds a clear, cool channel which empties into the Niangua River. The channel is well-stocked with trout and, on warm summer weekends, there seem to be more anglers than fish.

Named for Peter Bennett, who ran a grist mill along the Spring stream during the mid 1800s, the 3000 acre State Park is home to an excellent diversity of wildlife and harbors a fine network of trails. Hikers may encounter wild turkey, pileated woodpeckers, belted kingfishers, great blue herons, beaver, muskrat, mink and river otters here; nine-banded armadillos are relatively new residents in the Park, having wandered up from the south. Less conspicuous wildlife include southern redback salamanders, northern watersnakes, eastern hellbenders and the Niangue darter, an endangered species.

The Missouri Department of Conservation operates a **trout hatchery (H)** at Bennett Spring and the Park's **Nature Center (NC)** is well worth a visit; the latter houses natural history displays and operates educational programs throughout the year. The Nature Center is open daily during the summer months and Wednesday-Sunday from September through May.

Directions: From Lebanon, head west on Missouri 64. Drive almost 11 miles and turn left on Route 64-A. Proceed to parking areas as illustrated on the map. The hikes discussed in the guide begin at the **Nature Center (NC)**, at **Bennett Spring (BS)** and at the **Trailhead (TH)**.

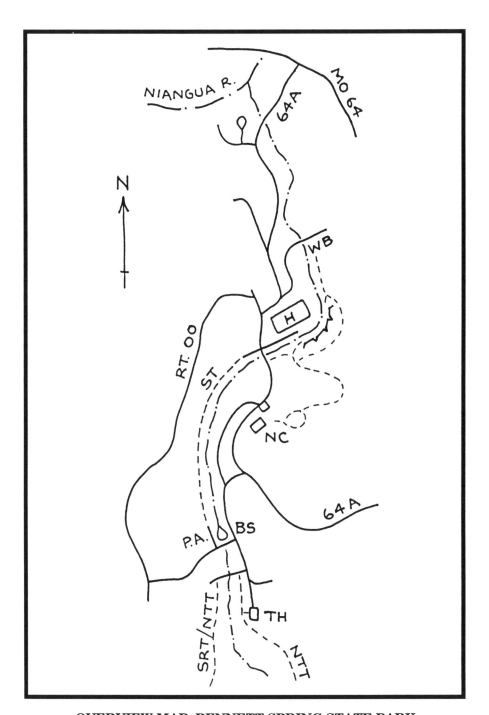

OVERVIEW MAP: BENNETT SPRING STATE PARK

Routes: Bennett Spring State Park offers 12 miles of hiking trails. We suggest the following dayhikes.

Spring Trail (ST). This wide path, illustrated on the overview map (page 145), parallels the Spring Branch from Bennett Spring (BS) to the Trout Hatchery (H). The roundtrip walk is 1.4 miles.

Nature Center Loop. A series of hiking trails, beginning just behind the Park's **Nature Center (NC)**, yields a hike of 1.5 miles. Enter the woods and bear left at the fork, passing the outdoor amphitheater (A). This arm of the **Oak-Hickory Trail (OHT)** curves gently up the ridge and soon intersects the **Bridge Trail (BRT)**. Turn left here, crossing a fine wooden bridge and then circling higher into the forest.

The Bridge Trail crosses the upper reaches of a drainage and then descends westward between two creek valleys. At the base of the ridge you will encounter a multi-trail junction where the Bridge Trail and **Bluff Trail (BLT)** intersect (see map). Turn right, cross the stream and climb onto the next ridge, soon hiking above rock bluffs that line the Spring Branch. A short stroll above these cliffs is followed by a steep descent into the next creek valley.

Descend via the rocky stairway and turn left, circling back beneath the rock bluffs and hiking along the waterway. Great blue and green-backed herons often fish along the stream and late-day visitors may spot a mink or river otter along the banks; otters were recently re-introduced to the Park.

Another stream crossing brings you back to the multi-trail intersection. Turn right and follow an arm of the **Bridge Trail (BRT)** out to the roadway (see map). Turn left and walk along the roadway to the Nature Center, completing a loop hike of 1.5 miles.

The Bridge Trail

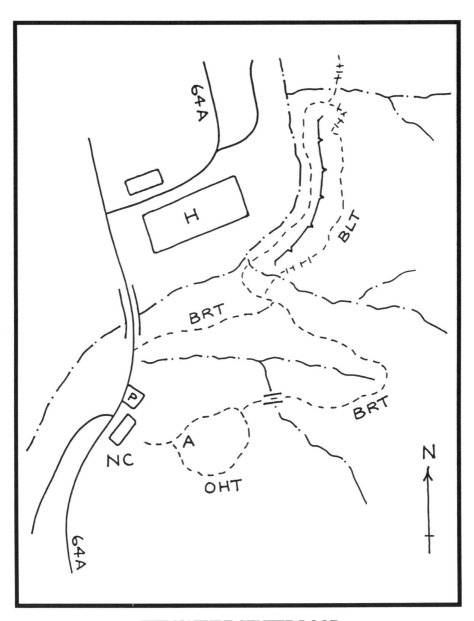

THE NATURE CENTER LOOP

Savanna Ridge Trail (SRT). This 2.5 mile loop hike begins and ends at the Trailhead lot (TH), a short distance south of Bennett Spring (see overview map on page 145). Hike northward from the lot and turn left on a graveled lane that crosses Spring Hollow Creek. Watch for the trail cutoff, on your left, before reaching the private residence; turn left here on a trail segment that is common to both the Savanna Ridge and Natural Tunnel Trails.

After hiking a short distance, the trail forks. Turn right on the Savanna Ridge Trail, blazed with green, and climb into the forest. As you hike this loop you will encounter clearings, known as dolomite glades, where thin, rocky soil retards forest invasion; watch for wild turkey and white-tailed deer in these openings. Other forest wildlife include eastern chipmunks, gray squirrels, eastern woodrats, gray fox, opossum and the rare bobcat.

Those wishing to shorten their route can use the White Connector Trail (WCT) which reduces the total hike to 1.5 miles. Either route will eventually bring you down to another junction with the **Natural Tunnel Trail (NTT)** which is blazed with blue. Turn left here and hike back to the Trailhead lot (see map).

Natural Tunnel Trail. This 7.5 mile loop hike begins and ends at the Trailhead lot (TH) a short distance south of Bennett Spring (see overview map on page 145). Hike northward from the lot, turn left on a graveled lane and cross Spring Hollow Creek. Once across the stream, turn left on the **Natural Tunnel Trail (NTT)**, which is blazed with blue; this first segment is also the entry route for the Savanna Ridge Trail, discussed above.

Bypass cutoffs to the **Savanna Ridge Trail (SRT)**, remaining in the creek valley. The trail eventually crosses a branch of Spring Hollow and soon thereafter reaches a junction where a **Connector Trail (CT)** offers a shortcut back to the Trailhead. The Natural Tunnel Trail continues southward, crosses another stream and climbs onto a ridge where evidence of an old homestead sits along the trail. The path zigzags across the ridge and then gradually descends to the valley floor, fording several creeks along the way. After crossing the main channel you will soon reach a trail junction.

Turn right (south) here, hiking across a broad meadow where blackberries grow in abundance. The trail eventually re-enters the forest where it crosses two pipeline swaths and a branch of Spring Hollow. Climbing a bit higher, the path crosses a low ridge, paralleling the stream, and then dips back to cross one of its tributaries; this is the creek that eroded the Natural Tunnel.

The trail turns eastward, crossing the stream five times before reaching the **Natural Tunnel (NT)**, a spectacular passage almost 300 feet long. The Tunnel, 15 feet high and 50 feet wide, was eroded from the thick, Ordovician dolomite by flowing water.

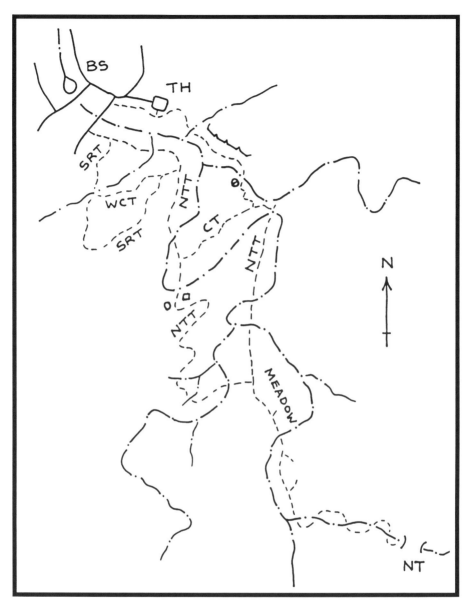

After enjoying this geologic wonder, retrace your path to the trail junction (just beyond the large meadow) and continue straight ahead, crossing Spring Hollow and passing through a smaller, wooded meadow. Another creek crossing brings you to a junction where a service road continues straight ahead; turn left here for a short but steep climb onto a ridge where the Connector Trail comes in from the west. Bear right, descending through the forest and recrossing Spring Hollow near a sinkhole. The Natural Tunnel Trail now angles to the northwest on a flat, rocky bed and, within .5 mile, emerges from the forest near the Trailhead lot.

APPENDIX I

THE NATURAL HISTORY OF MID MISSOURI

The scenic landscape of Central Missouri, its native wildlife and, indeed, the humans who explore, use and abuse it, are the culmination of 4.6 billion years of earth history. A knowledge of this past history will certainly add to your enjoyment of the hikes in this guide and, hopefully, will increase your commitment to protect what remains of our natural heritage.

PRECAMBRIAN ERA
4600-600 MYA*

The first four billion years of earth history were characterized by a gradual cooling of the planet's crust, relentless volcanic activity, formation of the atmosphere and evolution of the primordial seas. Life first evolved in these ancient oceans some 3.6 billion years ago, protected from the intense solar radiation by the nourishing seas themselves. By the end of the Precambrian Era, a tremendous diversity of marine invertebrates had evolved.

Precambrian rocks form the continental plates and underlie all of Missouri. Throughout the globe, these rocks are exposed where overlying sediments have been scraped away by glaciers (e.g. the Canadian Shield), where they have been pushed upward in mountain formations (e.g. the Rocky Mountains) or where rivers have cut deep canyons into the crust (e.g. the Grand Canyon). Precambrian rocks form the core of the Francois Mountains, a domal uplift in southeast Missouri; in other areas of the State, they have been covered by "younger" sedimentary rocks.

PALEOZOIC ERA
600-225 MYA

By the onset of the Paleozoic Era, the diversity of marine life was exploding. Brachiopods, bryozoans and trilobites reached their zenith during the **Cambrian (600-500 MYA)** and **Ordovician (500-440 MYA)** Periods. Shallow seas bathed much of North America during the Paleozoic Era, depositing limestones, dolomites, shales and sandstones on the Precambrian basement. **Cambrian rock** is exposed in the outer regions of the Francois Mountain uplift of southeastern Missouri and very late Cambrian dolomite, the Eminence Formation, can be seen at the base of the Ha Ha Tonka gorge.

*MYA - million years ago

150

Ordovician rocks are widespread acoss south-central and east-central Missouri. Gasconade dolomite, deposited in early Ordovician seas, is responsible for the spectacular karst topography of Bennett Spring, Ha Ha Tonka and Lake of the Ozarks State Parks. Graham Cave, itself the centerpiece of a State Park, is composed of middle Ordovician St. Peter Sandstone.

Bluffs of Ordovician dolomite line the Colosseum at Ha Ha Tonka State Park

During the **Silurian Period (440-400 MYA)**, the atmospheric ozone layer had thickened sufficiently to allow the first land plants to colonize coastal areas. Throughout the remainder of the Paleozoic, these pioneer plants would evolve into a remarkable diversity of ferns, horsetails and primitive conifers. Silurian sediments are exposed in limited areas of northeastern and southeastern Missouri. The **Devonian Period (400-350 MYA)**, witnessed the rise of sharks, bony fish, lung fish, primitive amphibians, ferns and the first tree-like plants; rocks of this period are exposed in the Missouri River bluffs of southern Boone, Callaway and Montgomery Counties.

The **Carboniferous Period (350-270 MYA)** was a time when extensive swamplands covered much of the globe. Giant amphibians and the first reptiles roamed these carbon-rich wetlands which would later decompose into thick beds of coal (e.g. the Appalachian coal fields). Geologists divide the Carboniferous Age into the **Mississippian (350-310 MYA)** and **Pennsylvanian (310-270 MYA)** Periods. Mississippian sedimentary rocks are exposed in a broad swath, from southwestern to northeastern Missouri. The Missouri River bluffs of Cooper and western Boone Counties are composed of Mississippian limestone (topped with glacial loess) and the Burlington Limestone of Rock Bridge State Park and greater Columbia, dates from this Period. The Salt River valley of northeastern

Mississippian limestone along Mark Twain Lake

Missouri, now covered by Mark Twain Lake, is also rimmed by Mississippian limestone.

Pennsylvanian sediments, a layer-cake of sandstones, limestones, shale and coal, underlie most of the Glaciated Plains of northern Missouri, the Osage Plains of western Missouri and a swath of the Ozark Plateau northwest of the Francois Mountains.

During the **Permian Period (270-225 MYA)**, earth's roaming continents merged, forming the land mass of **Pangea**. In the process, North America and Africa collided, crumpling the eastern end of the North American craton and forcing up the Appalachians. This uplift extended westward in the form of the **Ozark Plateau** and Quachita Mountains, which have since been carved into a maze of valleys and ridges by the numerous tributaries of the Missouri and Arkansas Rivers.

MESOZOIC ERA
(225-65 MYA)

Known as the Age of Reptiles, the **Mesozoic Era** witnessed the rise of the dinosaurs. Mesozoic sediments are rare in Missouri; only a few small areas of Cretaceous sandstone and clay dot the Coastal Plain of the Boot-Heel region. Geologists divide the Mesozoic into three Periods:

The **Tertiary Period (225-190 MYA)**, characterized by a hot, dry climate across much of the globe, gave rise to primitive crocodiles, turtles and small, herbivorous dinosaurs.

During the **Jurassic Period (190-135 MYA)**, conifers reached their evolutionary peak and flowering plants made their first appearance. Allosaurus, brontosaurus, stegasaurus and the pterysaurs ruled the Jurrasic while small, shrew-like creatures, the first mammals, evolved in relative obscurity. Early in the Period, Pangea split into **Laurasia** (North America-Europe-Asia) and **Gondwanaland** (Africa-Australia-Antarctica-South America); late in the Jurassic, Africa broke away from Gondwanaland and joined the Laurasian land mass.

Horned dinosaurs and Tyrannosaurus rex appeared in the **Cretaceous Period (135-65 MYA)**, during which a broad seaway covered much of central North America. Monotremes and marsupials evolved in Gondwanaland while primitive eutherians (placental mammals) spread across the northern Continents. By the end of the Mesozoic, a dramatic change in earth's environment, perhaps caused by a massive meteor strike, triggered extinction of the dinosaurs and set the stage for the rise of mammals.

CENOZOIC ERA
(65-0 MYA)

As the **Cenozoic Era** dawned, the Rocky Mountains were pushing skyward, creating a vast rain-shadow across the High Plains of North America. Drainage from these new Mountains created the Arkansas and Missouri Rivers, which were later fed by runoff from the Continental and Rocky Mountain glaciers. The Plains themselves, deprived of Pacific moisture by the Rockies, gave rise to a "sea of grass," which would later stretch from western Ohio to the foot of the mountains. More tolerant of wind and drought than are trees, these grasslands were also maintained by periodic wildfires as well as the trampling and grazing of huge bison herds. Eastern portions of these Great Plains, profitting from Gulf moisture and glacial till, were eventually covered by the rich, tallgrass prairie.

Periods of glaciation, which peaked during the **Pleistocene Epoch (2-.01 MYA)**, caused ocean levels to fall and opened land bridges between the Continents. These bridges, which developed and disappeared over thousands of years, allowed mammals to move between the Continents; primitive horses and camels travelled from North America to Asia across Beringea while bison and mammoths moved the opposite direction. In like manner, opossums, having evolved in South America, spread across the Isthmus of Panama into Central and North America.

Continental glaciers penetrated Missouri several times during the Pleistocene "Ice Age." The **Illinoin Glacier**, which crept south out of Canada some 400,000 years ago, molded the course of the Missouri River before retreating northward. The last ice sheet, the **Wisconsin Glacier**, invaded northern Missouri 70,000 years ago, scouring the till plains of America's Midwest and scooping out the beds of the five Great Lakes.

Man evolved in East Africa during the latter half of the Pleistocene and, by the end of the Epoch, had spread to all Continents except Antarctica. The first human Americans, having followed herds of bison and mammoth across the Bering land bridge, were likely south of the Wisconsin Glacier by 15-20,000 years ago. By the onset of the **Holocene (.01-0 MYA)**, these Paleo-hunters had adopted an **Archaic Culture**, with relatively permanent settlements. The **Dalton Period** (9-10,000 years ago) witnessed a transition to small game, foraging and regional communities; one of these Dalton communities was based at Graham Cave (see Hiking Area 15). The **Sedalia Culture**, appearing late in the Archaic, is known for hilltop settlements in southwest and northeast Missouri.

The **Woodland Period** (2400-3000 years ago) was heralded by pottery making and later encompassed the development of agriculture. The **Hopewell Culture**, known for earthworks throughout the Upper Mississippi and Ohio Valleys occupied parts of Missouri during the Woodland Period.

By the onset of the **Mississippi Period**, 3000 years ago, large, central communities communicated with outlying villages via trails and waterways; Cahokia, at the present location of St. Louis, was the largest of these centers. Modern tribal communities developed over the next 2000 years, with the **Osage** and **Oneota** Cultures forming in Missouri; the latter gave rise to the **Missouri Indians** who settled near the junction of the Grand and Missouri Rivers. Other tribes, including the Shawnee, the Iowa, the Kickapoo, the Illinois and the Delaware, settled in Missouri for brief periods of time.

When white explorers, trappers and traders first reached Missouri, they thus found a pristine landscape of forest, prairie and sparkling streams. Wildlife, including black bear, mountain lions, elk, wild turkey, eagles, beaver and river otter were abundant. Within two hundred years, most of the prairie had been converted to corn fields and the magnificent forests had been cleared for timber production, ranching mining and urban sprawl. Over-hunting and loss of habitat decimated the wildlife and industrial waste polluted the streams.

Due to the foresight and hard work of many conservation organizations, the tide has now turned and, for the past few decades, efforts have been underway to protect and restore native habitat. Endangered and threatened wildlife species are beginning to recover and extirpated species are being reintroduced. Nevertheless, pollution and development continue to stress the natural environment and conservation efforts are vital to the welfare of Missouri's open spaces. You can help to protect our natural heritage by contributing your time and/or money to the organizations listed in Appendix II.

APPENDIX II

REGIONAL CONSERVATION ORGANIZATIONS

The following is a partial list of conservation organizations that are working to protect Missouri's natural heritage. Your support for their effort will help to ensure the future welfare of the State's wild lands.

Audubon Society of Missouri, Hotline: 573-445-9115

Columbia Parks and Recreation, 1 South 7th St., Columbia, MO 65205
    573-874-7460, Hotline: 573-874-7663

Conservation Federation of Missouri, 728 W. Main, Jefferson City,
    MO 65101, 573-634-2322, 800-575-2322

Eastern National Forests Interpretive Association, 4549 State Rd. H,
    Fulton, MO 65251

Katy Trail Coalition, 1001 E. Walnut, #300, Columbia, MO 65201,
    573-443-1602

Katy Trail Volunteer Program, Missouri River District, Box 166,
    Boonville, MO 65233, 660-882-8196

Mark Twain National Forest, 401 Fairgrounds Rd., Rolla, MO 65401,
    314-364-4621; Cedar Creek Ranger District: 4549 State Rd. H,
    Fulton, MO 65251, 573-592-1400

Missouri Coalition for the Environment, 6267 Delmar, 2E, St. Louis,
    MO 63130, 314-727-0600, moenviron@aol.com

Missouri Department of Conservation, Box 180, Jefferson City, MO 65102
    www.conservation.state.mo.us
    Camdenton: 573-346-2210
    Clinton: 660-885-6981
    Columbia: 573-884-6861, 573-882-9880, 573-445-3882
    Fulton: 573-592-4080
    Grand River District: 816-646-6122
    Kirksville: 660-785-2420
    Lebanon: 417-532-7612
    Rolla: 573-368-2225
    Runge Conservation Nature Center: 573-526-5544
    Sullivan: 573-468-4157, 573-468-3335
    Williamsburg: 314-254-3330, 314-882-9880

Missouri Department of Natural Resources, Box 176, Jefferson City, MO 65102, 800-334-6946

Missouri Native Plant Society, Box 20073, St. Louis, MO 63144, 314-894-9021

Missouri Parks Association, Box 1811, Jefferson City, MO 65102
Membership: Box 42, Fulton, MO 65251

Missouri Prairie Foundation, Box 200, Columbia, MO 65205, 573-442-5842

Missouri Trails & Streams Association, Box 1478, Ballwin, MO 63021, 314-532-4742

The Nature Conservancy of Missouri, 2800 South Brentwood Blvd., St. Louis, MO 63144, 314-968-1105, www.tnc.org/missouri, email: missouri@tnc.org

Sierra Club, Ozark Chapter, 1007 N. College, Suite 1, Columbia, MO 65201 573-815-9250

Tucker Prairie Research Committee, Division of Biological Sciences, 110 Tucker Hall, University of Missouri, Columbia, MO 65211, 573-882-6659

BIBLIOGRAPHY

Beveridge, Thomas R., revised by Jerry D. Vineyard, **Geologic Wonders and Curiosities of Missouri**, 2nd Edition, Missouri Department of Natural Resources, Division of Geology & Land Survey, Rolla, 1990

Chapman, Carl H. and Eleanor F. Chapman, **Indians & Archaeology of Missouri**, Revised Edition, University of Missouri Press, Columbia, 1983

DeHaan, Vici, **State Parks of the Midwest: America's Heartland**, Johnson Books, Boulder, 1993

Dufur, Brett, **The Complete Katy Trail Guidebook**, 2nd Edition, Pebble Publishing, Columbia, 1996

Earngey, Bill, **Missouri Roadsides: the Traveler's Companion**, University of Missouri Press, Columbia, 1995

Flader, Susan (Editor), R. Roger Pryor, John A. Karel and Charles Callison, **Exploring Missouri's Legacy: State Parks & Historic Sites**, University of Missouri Press, Columbia and London, 1992

Johnson, Tom R., **The Amphibians & Reptiles of Missouri**, Missouri Department of Conservation, 1987, 1992, 1997

Palmer, Kay, compiler, **A Guide to Birding Areas of Missouri**, Audubon Society of Missouri, 1993

Robbins, Mark and David A. Easterla, **Birds of Missouri: Their Distribution and Abundance**, University of Missouri Press, 1991

Schwartz, Charles W. and Elizabeth R. Schwartz, **The Wild Mammals of Missouri**, University of Missouri Press and the Missouri Department of Conservation, Revised Edition, 1981

Thompson, Thomas L. and Charles E. Robertson, **Guidebook to the Geology along Interstate Highway 44 (I-44) in Missouri**, Missouri Department of Natural Resources, Division of Geology & Land Survey, Rolla, 1993

Unklesbay, A.G. and Jerry D. Vineyard, **Missouri Geology: Three Billion Years of Volcanoes, Seas, Sediments & Erosion**, University of Missouri Press, 1992

White, Louis C., **Ozark Hideaways**, University of Missouri Press, Columbia and London, 1993

Winters, Sally & Sharon Kinney Hanson, **Katy Trail: Jefferson City to Boonville**, Sheba Review Publishing, Jefferson City, 1992

INDEX

The Index in this guide is a Functional Index. Rather than relisting all of the natural areas, trails, persons and wildlife that are mentioned in the book, we have categorized the information. We hope that this will serve to direct readers to those areas that might be of special interest to them. Wildlife listings are limited to uncommon species or those mammals and birds which are unique to certain habitats.

lakes, large - 3, 7, 9, 13, 17, 37, 38
lakes, woodland - 5, 8, 29, 32, 33

mink - area 40
Mississippian rock exposures - areas 19, 21, 22, 26

natural bridges/tunnels - areas 21, 38, 40
nature centers - areas 5, 30, 37, 38, 40

Ordovician rock exposures - areas 15, 31, 37, 38, 40
osprey - areas 7, 11, 17, 23
otter, river - areas 1, 2, 40
overlooks - areas 6, 19, 22, 24, 31, 34, 35, 37, 38, 40
owl, barred - see floodplain woodlands
owl, great horned - see upland forest

pelican, American white - 3, 4, 7, 23
prairie habitat - areas 2, 19-21, 30, 37
prehistoric sites - areas 5, 15, 31

quarries, abandoned - areas 18, 38

rail-to-trail conversions - areas 20, 26
rivers/large creeks - 9. 11, 15, 19, 23-26, 29, 31, 34, 39, 40

salamander, southern redback - area 40
savannas - areas 38, 40
shorebirds, migrant - areas 3, 4, 7, 23
sinkholes - areas 21, 38, 40
springs - areas 21, 38, 40
State Natural Areas - 2, 37
State Parks - 2, 5, 9, 15, 21, 37, 38, 40
swan, trumpeter - area 23

trails, long (over 5 miles) - areas 2, 3, 9, 14, 20, 25, 26, 29, 37, 40
trails, paved or graded - areas 17, 20, 26, 38
trout hatchery - area 40
turkey, wild - see upland forest and floodplain woodlands

waterfowl, migrant - areas 1, 3, 4, 17, 23
wetlands - areas 1-4, 7, 18, 20, 23
woodpecker, pileated - see upland forest
woodpecker, red-headed - see floodplain woodlands